My Escape
from
Donington Hall

Kapitänleutnant Gunther Plüschow

My Escape
from
Donington Hall

Gunther Plüschow

Pen & Sword
MILITARY

First published in Great Britain in 2015 by
Pen & Sword Military
an imprint of
Pen & Sword Books Ltd
47 Church Street
Barnsley
South Yorkshire
S70 2AS

ISBN 978 1 47382 705 9

A CIP catalogue record for this book is available from the British
Library

Typeset in Ehrhardt by
Mac Style Ltd, Bridlington, East Yorkshire
Printed and bound in the UK by CPI Group (UK) Ltd,
Croydon, CRO 4YY

Pen & Sword Books Ltd incorporates the imprints of Pen &
Sword Archaeology, Atlas, Aviation, Battleground, Discovery,
Family History, History, Maritime, Military, Naval, Politics,
Railways, Select, Transport, True Crime, and Fiction, Frontline
Books, Leo Cooper, Praetorian Press, Seaforth Publishing and
Wharncliffe.

For a complete list of Pen & Sword titles please contact
PEN & SWORD BOOKS LIMITED
47 Church Street, Barnsley, South Yorkshire, S70 2AS, England
E-mail: enquiries@pen-and-sword.co.uk
Website: www.pen-and-sword.co.uk

Contents

List Of Illustrations

Introduction

Gunther Plüschow (1886–1931) has the unique distinction of being the only German serviceman to escape from a Prisoner of War camp in the British Isles and make a 'home run' to Germany in either of the two world wars; indeed, only one other (Franz von Werra) managed to do so from any Prisoner of War camp, which he achieved in the Second World War from Canada via the USA and Mexico.

Plüschow lived an extraordinary life, culminating in his death as the result of an air crash in the Argentine part of Patagonia at the age of forty-four.

He was serving in the Imperial German Navy as a recently commissioned flyer at the outbreak of the war and was based in the German enclave in China of Tsingtau (modern Qindao). A little over a third of the book is taken up with a description of his exploits there, the attempts to keep his aircraft airworthy (it was the only one the defenders had) and the story of the defence of this German outpost against Japanese Imperial forces, which continued into November 1914. This part of the book alone makes it highly unusual, as first-hand accounts of these German outposts of empire in the war are few and far between. He was ordered to fly out of the enclave before it fell and get back to Germany as best he could; this he almost achieved (crashing his aircraft in the process).

He had various adventures in China and managed to make his way, armed with papers in Shanghai that identified him as Swiss, to the west coast of the USA and from there to New York. The next stage was to get to Italy (at this time still neutral), but he was identified in Gibraltar and thus the first stage of his bid to return to the Fatherland had resulted in failure.

He was imprisoned in the fairly relaxed camp regime of Donington Hall, in Leicestershire, in May 1915. He escaped on 4 July and after some time in London, he foiled attempts to board shipping heading for neutral ports – often spending nights hiding in the British Museum – he managed to get on a ferry, the SS *Prinses Juliana*, heading for the Netherlands. On 12 July he was in Germany – though at first no one believed his story and he was suspected of being a spy. He met the Emperor shortly afterwards and was awarded the Iron Cross First Class and was promoted.

A convinced monarchist, he felt very uncomfortable in post-war Germany and engaged in a number of failed attempts to set up a business. He began his new career of aviation explorer in South America via working on a merchant ship, leaving behind for long periods of time his extraordinarily supportive wife, Isot – whom he married in 1916 – and his young son, Guntolf (who in later life took his father's Christian name).

Discovering the wonders of photography and able to finance himself by writing, he was able to return to his first love and take once more to the skies in a flying boat, becoming a pioneer in aerial photography. It was whilst engaged in this in January 1931 that he crashed near El Calafate, just inside the Argentinian border, and he and his companion, Ernst Dreblow, were killed. His remains were cremated and returned to Germany, to be joined by those of Isot in 1979.

Fortunately there is a recent biography of Plüschow: *Gunther Plüschow: Airman, Escaper, Explorer*, by Anton Rippon (Pen & Sword Books, 2009).

Escape from Donington Hall is not a literary masterpiece by any means; but it is a real 'boy's own' story and the reader gets a clear picture of the mentality of an intensely patriotic German officer. The language and the manner in which the patriotism is expressed are, of course, of the time. Direct comparisons can be made with British officers in a similar situation, such as that portrayed in *I Escaped*, the memoir of Jocelyn Hardy, an officer in the Connaught Rangers, captured in August 1914, which recounts his numerous escapes from German Prisoner of War camps (also published by Pen & Sword, 2014).

Nigel Cave

Chapter One

The Joys and Sorrows of a Flying-Man

It was in the month of August of the year 1913 when I arrived in my native town, Schwerin. I had stayed several weeks in England, where I had devoted days to the visit of museums and the beautiful art collections, as well as to excursions in the vicinity of the capital. At that time I did not foresee how useful the latter would prove to me two years hence.

During the whole journey I was labouring under an inner excitement and disquiet which I could not throw off, and when I arrived in Schwerin one question only burned on my lips, and yet I did not dare put it to my uncle who fetched me from the station. For the new Naval List of autumn promotions and appointments might be issued any day, and I was on the tiptoe of expectation as to whether the wish I had cherished for years was at last to be gratified.

My uncle's question: "Do you know where they've put you?" gave me an electric shock.

"No."

"Well, then, hearty congratulations – Naval Flying Corps!"

I was so overjoyed that I would like to have turned a somersault in the middle of the street, but I refrained from fear of upsetting my fellow-citizens.

So I had got my wish after all!

The last days of my leave passed in a flash, and I gaily returned to the Naval College in order to complete my course of a year and a half as Inspecting Officer; but I never packed my trunks with greater pleasure than when bound for my new destination.

Just a few days before my departure one of my brother officers called out to me: "I say, have you heard the latest news where you're off to?"

"Yes; Flying Corps."

"Good Lord, man! You don't know your own luck – why, you're off to Kiao-Chow."

I was speechless, and probably looked as stupid as I felt.

"Yes; Kiao-Chow! And in the Flying Corps! You lucky devil – to be the First Naval Flying Officer at Kiao-Chow!"

It is hardly surprising that I refused to believe this until I received the official confirmation. But it was true. I had tremendous luck!

I had to wait three months longer at Kiel; but at last, on the 1st of January 1914, I found myself in my beloved Berlin. But there was no holding me; I was at Johannisthal on the 2nd of January already, and thought I could start flying on the spot. My experience, however, was that of the majority of flying-pupils. I learnt for the first time the time – honoured principle of flight: "Keep cool; who wants to fly must above all things learn to wait."

Wait, wait, and once more wait. Eighty per cent of the science of flying consists in waiting and holding oneself in readiness.

Winter had come and covered the aerodrome with a deep, white carpet, making flying impossible. For weeks every morning I had the hope that the snow would melt at last, and every afternoon I returned home disappointed.

In February at last the weather changed. On the 1st of February I sat happily in my Taube, and for the first time rose into the glorious clear winter air. It was beautiful now; and every day our schooling progressed.

Flying suited me, and I grasped it quickly. And I was very proud that on the third day I was allowed to fly alone. Two days later, on a beautiful Saturday afternoon, my untiring instructor, Werner Wieting, asked me whether I would not care to create a nice little record by passing my examination as pilot. I enthusiastically agreed.

Ten minutes later I sat in my machine, circling gaily in the prescribed curves. It was a real joy to keep going in the lovely winter air. And when I achieved a perfect landing, which concluded my examination, and my teacher proudly shook me by the hand and congratulated me, I felt extremely happy and filled with a sensation of inner satisfaction.

At last I was a pilot. The school-stage was over, and from now onwards I could fly daily on one of the big 100 h.p. machines.

One particular undertaking was to be the source of much pleasure to me. Rumpler had just completed a monoplane which was specially designed for climbing. It now became our aim to achieve a high-altitude flight record. The famous pilot, Linnekogel, was to fly the machine, and he asked me to accompany him as observer. It was only natural that I accepted with delight.

On one of the last days in February we started on our first trial trip. Warmly wrapped up against the severe cold, we sat in our machine, and many eyes followed us with envy as our bird rose in the air with the lightness of a dragon-fly. Watch in hand, I noted the altitude, and after fifteen minutes we had already reached 2000 metres, which at that time was considered an extraordinarily good performance. But after that we only progressed slowly. The atmosphere became bumpy, and we were flung about like feathers by violent eddies or bumps. After an hour we had at last reached 4000 metres, when with a popping and spluttering noise the motor began to run irregularly, and stopped altogether after a few seconds. We now descended in spirals towards the earth, and some minutes later the machine stood unharmed on the flying-ground.

The cold had been too great, and the motor was simply frozen – a circumstance which nobody had foreseen. New improvements were promptly added. After a few days we started again on the same adventure, but this time better luck seemed in store for us. We climbed steadily and securely 4000 metres, 4200, 4500 metres. Thank God, our last record was broken! The cold was well-nigh unbearable, and I am convinced that the thickest hide would have been no protection against it.

4800, 4900 metres! 400 more and our object was attained. But the machine seemed bewitched, and refused to climb another metre! All our attempts to induce an extra effort failed. We were running short of petrol, and the engine gave out completely this time.

An altitude of 4900 metres! We landed, without a single drop of petrol, nearly frozen to ice. We had not achieved all we had set out to do; however, it was a good result. We had won, and won brilliantly, the German high-altitude record.

But success made us ambitious. At the beginning of March weather conditions again improved sufficiently to allow us to try our luck once more. More warmly clad than last time, and fitted out with thermometers, though without an oxygen apparatus, we started on our third attempt.

We reached the first altitude with ease. The sky was covered with huge clouds, the air icy. When we rose through the bank of clouds into the glorious sunshine we had a beautiful experience. We suddenly saw a radiantly shining Zeppelin, which was likewise attempting a flight at high altitude.

What a marvellous meeting – 3000 metres up in the air! Far away from toiling humanity, high up above daily strife and pain, the two birds of the air – striking evidence of Germany's strength and enterprise – saluted each other.

We flew several times round our big brother, and waved our hand to him in friendly greeting.

But after that we had to apply ourselves seriously to our task and work strenuously in order to attain our objective. After an hour we had gained an altitude of 4800 metres, after that 4900, my barograph soon showed 5000, and the propeller hummed its monotonous melody. Linnekogel veered quietly and methodically. The thermometer rose to 37 degrees Celsius; but we paid no attention to the cold. Only the air became rarefied. A slight sensation of drowsiness came over me, and my lungs only functioned in quick, short gasps. Every movement became irksome. Even to turn round towards the pilot who sat behind me seemed a huge effort.

The sky had cleared and looked glorious. The cloud-banks had vanished, and we could distinguish our capital lying far below us in the blue distance like a black spot, on which, however, we could still note the straight line of the Charlottenburger Chaussee, culminating in the thoroughfare Unter den Linden.

I was so carried away by this view that for some time I paid no attention to either watch or barograph. But I suddenly realized my omission with a start. Twenty minutes had passed since I had registered my barograph at 5000 metres, and by now we should have beaten our record. But I was terribly disappointed to see that the needle still indicated 5000. At the same time, Linnekogel began signalling to me to look for the aerodrome, pointing downwards with his hand. That was too bad. I turned away disgustedly, and, when Linnekogel failed to notice it, I kicked his shin with none too much gentleness. I likewise spread out my five fingers and pointed upwards. This meant: Higher, higher! We have only got to 5000 metres!

Linnekogel only laughed. He gripped my hand, shook it hard, and opened and shut the five fingers of his right hand twice. I really thought he had gone dotty. And what confirmed me in my opinion was that Linnekogel throttled the engine. We were just above Potsdam, and glided towards the aerodrome of Johannisthal. It was now my job to find the landing-place. And sixteen minutes later we stood safe and sound before the Rumpler-hangars, joyfully acclaimed by crowds of spectators.

We had done it! The world's record was broken with 5500 metres.

The flight had only lasted an hour and three quarters in all. We stood proudly amongst our less fortunate fellow-mortals who had remained on terra firma. Linnekogel was right. My barograph had frozen, whilst his – better protected – resisted the high temperature.

The days passed, and the time came when I had to leave my country.

My Taube, which had been specially constructed for Kiao-Chow, neared its completion, and with a curious feeling I took it out on its trial flight, after it had fulfilled the requisite conditions for acceptance. I was conscious that it was the most beautiful flying-machine in the world.

But my ambition was not yet realized. It seemed imperative that before I left for the Far East I should carry out an important overland flight in Germany.

I was lucky. My request met with ready response from Herr Rumpler, and he kindly allowed me the use of one of his aeroplanes for a several days' flight over Germany. I quickly passed my examination as field-pilot, and at the end of March, one fine morning at 7 a.m., I sat in my well-equipped Taube, and in the seat in front of me, tall and slim, my good friend Oberleutnant Strehle of the War Academy as observer.

It was the first time he had ever been in an aeroplane. But I think he will never forget his first flight as long as he lives.

We started brilliantly. And proudly I took off, until having reached an altitude of 500 metres I proceeded in a northerly direction. Everything went well. We passed over the Havel lakes, sighted Nauen; but suddenly the atmosphere became thick and murky and our bad luck set in. We were wrapped in a thick fog and could see nothing of the ground. For the first overland flight of my young life it was a tall order. But, with the fine confidence of the novice, I consoled myself with the thought that courage was-everything – even if things couldn't help getting worse! And I flew calmly into the thick fog, directing myself by my compass towards the north, as our objective was Hamburg. After, two hours we could make out the ground again at a distance of 300 metres below us, and who can describe our joy on espying a beautiful, large, ploughed field! I glided down gently, just as though it were an aerodrome, and landed safe and sound in the middle of the field. People came running from all sides, and my joy was great when I learned that we were on good Mecklenburg soil, and exactly where, according to my own and my observer's calculations, we had expected to find ourselves. It was a holiday, and we afforded the villagers a free entertainment.

As soon as it cleared up, we decided to depart. But the soft soil held the wheels fast, and it was impossible to rise. With shrieks of merriment, and many a rough jest which we had to accept, the willing spectators trundled the giant bird over the field.

After we had cut down a few trees, we had to negotiate a ditch and another field. Though we now intended to depart, we were only allowed to do so after partaking of most excellent coffee and pound-cake.

After a mighty hand shaking all round, and shouting themselves hoarse with endless " Hurrahs", with much waving of handkerchiefs, we started off on a northerly course.

But our joy was short-lived, for fifteen minutes later we were again in the midst of grey fog-banks. After two hours I found the situation getting unpleasant, for the confounded motor began to choke and spit, and was either 500 revolutions short or registered 200 too many.

I examined my landing-gear and valves, and noticed to my horror that my provision of petrol was diminishing with hideous rapidity. I kept my machine balanced as well as possible, and glided down to a height of 300 metres.

But, oh, Lord! The mist lifted a little and I could see where I was – exactly over the river Alster at only 300 metres' altitude, and this with a motor that was running dry, and with no idea where to look for the aerodrome of Fuhlsbüttel. There was only one thing to do – and that was to keep calm and cool! Above all, to get away from the town and thus avoid imperilling human lives. I pencilled these words on a scrap of paper and passed them to my observer: "We must land within five minutes or we shall take a cold bath, as we have no more petrol." He peered about him and suddenly pointed joyfully to a cemetery which lay right under us. Good old chap! He had no idea of our predicament and could not guess what unconscious irony lay behind his gesture.

We had already dropped 200 metres. The engine was working by fits and starts; the level of the petrol showed 10 litres. But I was pleased. For we had now left the town behind us, and though a smooth landing was impossible, amongst all these suburban gardens, at least I hoped to avoid killing anyone. At such times every second seems an eternity, and my thoughts chased each other across my brain. But more than ever I had to show iron determination and self-control.

My observer suddenly started waving his hand and pointing forwards. And even now I can see his sparkling eyes shining at me through his goggles.

The sheds of the Fuhlsbüttel aerodrome, shimmering in the rays of the setting sun faintly encircled by the mist, lay before us.

Hurrah! We were saved.

Who can describe my joy? With my last litre of petrol I described a loop round the aerodrome and, gliding down in a steep spiral, landed.

I nearly fell on my observer's neck, so happy did I feel. The dear old chap had no inkling of the danger in which we had been, and was very surprised when I told him about it. Even now, when I know what flying means, I go cold when I think of this first flight. I soon found out what had happened. The lower part of the carburettor was damaged, and the petrol leaked through the fracture with each throb of the engine. This also explained the rapid sinking of the petrol and the irregular working of the engine. To this day I cannot understand why there was no fire.

After spending three days with dear friends in Bremen the new carburettor arrived in Hamburg. Now, we wanted to move on to our next destination – Schwerin in Mecklenburg.

On a rainy, stormy afternoon we settled ourselves in our fully equipped aeroplane. I started the engine and took on full throttle.

Today I would only fly in such weather if I absolutely could not help it. But at that time I was still imbued with all the *naïveté* and enthusiasm of a young pilot. But we had not long to wait for new developments. The machine, which was too heavily freighted, could not rise – gusts of wind threw it from side to side like a ball – and I would have turned back with pleasure. But at that height it was impossible.

And now came the first houses of Hamburg – it was impossible to rise above them. I was flying at 60 metres when I saw a small field. Throttling my engine, I got ready to land, but at the same moment

I was caught in a squall and felt the aeroplane slide away under me. The thought went through my mind, "Careful, you are falling!" and I opened up my engine momentarily in order to weaken the shock. But at the same moment I felt a sharp jerk, and the machine stood on its head as if some one were tilting it downwards.

What followed only took seconds. I pulled at my lever, shut off the petrol, and at the same time received a sharp, heavy blow. I clutched convulsively at my steering-wheel, and flew into the air, hitting my head against some part of the machine.

A deathly silence reigned around me.

Deep darkness; from which I was only roused by feeling a stream of pungent liquid pouring over my face.

I lay motionless, my head pressed forward, my body huddled together, feet sticking out. But suddenly I realized my position with a start, and, obsessed by the fear of the machine catching fire at any moment, I tried to free myself from my cramped position, until I succeeded in switching off the ignition. At last I gradually regained complete consciousness of my surroundings, and my first thought was for my poor observer. I felt sure that as he sat in front he must have borne the brunt of the first shock and was probably crushed to a pulp, as the fuselage had splintered under the impact. As no sound broke the silence, I gasped at last – for I was so squeezed in that I could hardly breathe: "Strehlchen, are you alive?"

A dreadful pause; no answer.

On repeating my question, I heard at last: "I say, what has happened? It is quite dark here – something *must* have happened!"

Ah, how glad I was! I shouted with the rest of my strength: "Strehlchen, man, you are still alive – that's all that matters! What about your bones? Are they whole?" But the poor chap was lying so huddled up that he was only able to gasp: "I don't know. We'll see later on!"

Again silence supervened. The petrol flowed in a rich stream from the tank, which held its full capacity of 170 litres; but after a time, which seemed an eternity, somebody knocked outside, and a far away voice floated to where we lay: "Well, anybody still alive?"

"Rather," I called out, "but hurry up, or we shall suffocate in here."

We heard the machine being lifted, then the grating of spades, and at last a current of fresh air blew in on us.

"Hold hard!" shouted Strehle. "Try the other way round or you'll break my arm."

Our helpers followed my instructions, and at last I was lifted clear from my seat, and I lay softly and at ease on an odorous manure heap. Long-legged Strehle promptly clambered out of the debris, and I have rarely shaken hands with more pleasure than with my faithful observer.

Dash it all! Things did look bad. The machine had completely toppled over, and was deeply embedded in the soft manure. The fuselage was broken in three places; the planes had turned into a tangled mass of wood, fabric and wire.

But we two were safely out of it. Strehle had sprained his back slightly, and I had only broken two ribs. That was all. Never again have I despised a manure heap. May that one and its like flourish for ever. Sadly and limpingly we covered the rest of the return journey by train. After that, however, we enjoyed many days of sunshine and light, full of happy doings and happier memories, which we collected like flowers of rare beauty and bloom.

And then duty called, and the real voyage began.

Chapter Two

Beautiful Days in Kiao-Chow

For days the train took me farther and farther through the steppes and desert spaces of Russia towards my destination – the Far East.

Mukden at last! We soon passed Peking. Then – Osinanfou! The first German sounds again smote upon my ear. And then for ten hours we passed through a beautifully cultivated country full of gardens, fields and flowers; and at last the train slowly steamed into the station of Kiao-Chow.

I thus saw it again after six years! Once more I stood on German soil, in a German city of the Far East!

My brother officers met me. The Mongolian ponies pranced off and carried me to my new home.

At first we went to Iltis Place, which was our race course, and was at the same time destined to become my aerodrome. It was festively decorated, for all Kiao-Chow had foregathered to watch a big football match between German sailors and their English comrades from the English flagship *Good Hope*.

The latter was on a visit at Kiao-Chow, and the game was brilliant and ended in a draw – one all.

Who could have foreseen this? A short six months hence these same adversaries opposed each other in a terrible game, which admitted but of two issues – victory or death. At the battle of Coronel the German bluejackets sent the English flagship *Good Hope* to her doom at the bottom of the Pacific in twenty seven minutes.

But on that day none knew of the events to come and, united by bonds of sincere friendship, the German sailors invited their English guests to their cantonments. Two days later the English Squadron left our port followed by our Cruiser Squadron under Admiral Count von Spee.

The flags fluttered gaily in the wind, conveying the signals of the two admirals in command: "Farewell – until we meet again!"

Who could foresee that it would be at Coronel?

Immediately after my arrival, and after I had reported myself officially, I looked round for my aeroplane, in hopes of being able to show the amazed citizens of Kiao-Chow my beautiful giant bird. But—!

I had to curb my eagerness, for my machine was sailing jauntily round India and the steamer only due in July. "What can't be cured must be endured," I said to myself, and now had plenty of time to look round Kiao-Chow and to choose a house. A delightful little villa, quite close to the flying-ground, stood vacant, and I promptly took possession of it with my new comrade, Patzig. I had everything now to make me happy: my excellent billet at Kiao-Chow – this paradise on earth – work after my own heart, and, to cap it all, this charming residence, perched high on an eminence, with a lovely view on to Iltis Place and the distant, dark blue sea. Apart from this, I belonged to the Cavalry Detachment, and three happy years lay before me. Who could be more contented than I? I now set about arranging my house. I had a great number of plates on interior decoration, and with these I visited a Chinese cabinetmaker and ordered the furniture. It is marvellous with how much skill the Chinese are able to imitate our models, in what a short time, and how cheaply. When, four weeks later, everything was shipshape, the different pieces standing in their proper places, and the whole house shining with cleanliness, the masters of the house proudly took possession of their new abode. Nothing was lacking. Even servants were provided. If a European wishes to stand well with the Chinese, he must surround himself with a considerable number of Chinese servants; and one may affirm it is practically the moral duty of every European to do so.

Maurice, the cook, in his lovely blue silken Ishang; Fritz, the Mafu (groom), a perpetual grin on his face, but very concerned about the welfare of his horses; Max, the gardener, as lazy as a slug; and August, the pert little "boy", composed our staff.

To this must be added "Herr" Dorsch and "Herr" Simon.

These two gentlemen were our batmen, who took the fullest advantage of the custom of the Far East, that a European must do no manual labour in the presence of a Chinese.

Our house was surrounded by a big garden, which also contained the stables, the coach house, the garage and the huts of the Chinese. To me the most important was my hen coop. As soon as I arrived I bought myself a sitting hen, gave her a dozen eggs to hatch, and when we entered our house we already had seven chickens.

Poultry is cheap in China. The hen cost fourpence, a duck or a goose a shilling, and in a short time I had a poultry yard of fifty birds.

And, as I had also become a cavalryman, I had, of course, acquired a horse. One of my friends had a ripping little roan. We soon clinched our bargain, and "Fips" was transferred to my stables. "Fips" was a delightful animal, a good service-horse, yet excellent for hunting and polo, which did not prevent him from leaving me in the lurch at the beginning of the Kiao-Chow siege. I had ridden out into the territory the day before we were shut up in the fortress, and he took fright at some shrapnel which burst close to us, and so ran over to the enemy.

Life in the East was very monotonous for the Europeans. Very little socially, no music, no theatre – things one misses. One's only consolation is that one lives better than at home, and sport makes up for a great deal. I took up polo with enthusiasm, and as soon as I had accustomed myself to the unusual pitching and tossing to which my horse subjected me I was very successful.

In mid-July my longing was stilled by the arrival of the steamer which brought the aeroplanes. As soon as the huge crates stood in the quay, my men were already engaged in freeing from their dark prisons my poor birds born for sunshine and air. As they were too heavy, the unpacking had to be done on the spot. The Chinese crowd stood around us and gaped. When we had got everything out of the crates, a triumphal procession was formed, bearing the two aeroplanes, then three vehicles with the planes and another two with the component parts. The horses started, and we proudly passed through the streets of Kiao-Chow, and entered in triumph the aerodrome of the Iltis Place.

Now there was an end to peace. Day and night we worked at the erection of the machine and, two days later, in the early dawn, with no one awake, my aeroplane stood ready on the aerodrome and, opening up the engine full, I shot into the clear sea-air.

I shall never forget my first flight at Kiao-Chow. The aerodrome was extraordinarily small, only 600 metres long and 200 metres wide, full of obstacles, surrounded by hills and rocks. I was only to learn later how very difficult starting and landing were made hereby. My friend Clobuczar, an Austrian ex-aviator – who now served on the *Kaiserin Elisabeth* – once said to me: "Do you call this an aerodrome? It is at best a children's playground. I have never seen anyone who could fly in such a confined place." I felt the same way about it. And in Germany I should have only used it for an emergency landing.

But nothing could be done. It was the one place in the whole Protectorate; all the rest was composed of wild mountains cleft by deep ravines. But on that glorious, sunny morning I only thought of my flight, and frightened the placid inhabitants of Kiao-Chow out of their beauty sleep with the humming of my propeller. But, when it came to landing, I certainly felt a little queer, for the field was decidedly small, and I slowly circled round, getting gradually lower – thus putting off the critical moment. However, I could not stay up in the air for ever, so I pulled myself together, shut off the engine, and stood on the field a moment later after a secure landing. Now I knew where I was. And the rest of the morning was spent in my aeroplane.

After that more work was in store for me. The second machine, also a Rumpler-Taube, which was to be flown by my colleague, Leutnant Müllerskowski, of the battalion of Marines, had to be erected and got into working order. After two days, on the 31st of July 1914, it was ready in the afternoon. Müllerskowski entered his aeroplane and, after receiving my parting instructions based on my previous experience of the flying-field, he took off.

But fortune did not smile on him.

His machine was only a few seconds in the air, and had just reached an altitude of 50 metres – the critical spot where the aerodrome and solid earth end in a steep cliff with a sheer drop into the sea – when it suddenly turned over on the wing, and we could watch it nosing down with appalling rapidity towards the rocks.

We hastened as fast as we could to the spot. Matters looked bad. The machine was completely wrecked, and between the fragments we found Müllerskowski. We brought him, seriously injured, to the hospital, where he had to lie until shortly before the end of the siege. Of the aeroplane nothing remained.

In the meanwhile July had come, and brought with it the loveliest weather, most radiant sunshine, and the bluest of skies. It was Kiao-Chow's best month.

The bathing season was at its height. There were many charming ladies, mostly from the European and American settlements in China and Japan, visiting the "Ostend of the Far East" and enjoying the beauty of Kiao-Chow.

Amusement was the order of the day.

Motor drives, riding-parties, polo and tennis filled the free hours, and in the evenings dancing held undisputed sway. There were many Englishwomen amongst the women, and our relations were most pleasant and cordial.

For the beginning of August we had challenged the English Polo Club at Shanghai to a match when, on the 30th of July – like a bolt from the blue – came the order warning us of "Danger of war!"

Chapter Three

Threat of War – My Taube

I remember it as if it were yesterday. In the early hours of the morning an orderly arrived at our villa and brought Patzig and myself the order to report at once to the Divisional Commander, as "Protection" had been ordered. We naturally imagined this only to be a manoeuvre, and grumblingly repaired to our rendezvous. But there we received confirmation of the hardly credible news. And, with doubt still in our hearts, we hastened to our batteries and began the necessary preparations.

The order, "Threatening danger of war", which arrived next day, brought us certainty at last. It was followed on the 1st of August by the mobilization, on the 2nd by the declaration of war against Russia, and on the 3rd by that against France.

It is impossible to describe those days. And for this reason: here we were, a German Colony, a German fortress, the greater proportion of the Kiao-Chow population consisting of officers and soldiers. Moreover, to judge by externals, Kiao-Chow had become international. Russians, French and English lived with us as our guests. It was a cross-current of opinions and feelings, such as could hardly have been found elsewhere.

The main question – I should like to say *the* question – which occupied all our minds was: Will there be war with England? Only those who have lived in the East can judge what this question meant to us.

On the 2nd of August we were informed of our offer to England. I rode out that day with an English lady, and it was natural that this subject should form the chief topic of conversation. My companion's opinion, as that of all her friends, was that a war between England and Germany was unthinkable, as it would sound the death-knell of the prestige of the white race, and give the yellow Jap the opportunity of gathering the fruits of our dissension.

Our minds, of course, were filled with this contingency. The tension was even worse than during the first days of mobilization. And when, on the 4th of August, we got the news that war had been declared against England, it came as a deliverance – the die was cast in Europe!

It is impossible to pretend that we felt particularly happy: quite the contrary. Again and again we remembered that we were far away in Kiao-Chow, whilst at home those lucky devils, our brothers and comrades, were rejoicing to the full in the glorious days of mobilization. *They* were going to war against a world of enemies, *they* were to be allowed to defend our holy and beloved Fatherland, their wives and children, whilst we sat here, powerless to help! The thought alone was enough to drive us mad. For we knew that neither English, Russian nor French, by whom we were so greatly outnumbered, would find the courage to attack us here. However, the hope persisted: "Perhaps they will!" Oh, what a warm reception we would have given them!

Of course no one for a moment thought of Japan!

In the midst of all the work which the days of mobilization brought in their wake, we did not forget our guests. Nearly all of them were enemies, but they remained our guests.

Their excitement was comprehensible. The more so, as news of the absolutely brutal treatment of the Germans by the English in the British Colonies was already reaching us.

It was natural that we should break off our relations with the foreigners, but it was also a matter of course – and I should particularly like to point this out to the English – that all foreign subjects were treated with a consideration to be expected from "Huns" alone.

The foreigners were informed that they could stay on or depart from Kiao-Chow without any let or hindrance, and that the Governor would give them due warning at what time they would be expected to leave the Colony. It was only requested that no one should move beyond the confines of the city, go near the fortifications, or carry on espionage. Let who will compare this with the behaviour of our dear cousins at Hong Kong and so many other places in the world. All who went through these experiences could write volumes about them. One consolation remained to us: the daily wireless from home!

It is difficult to depict the delight with which we received this news. Usually the telegrams arrived in the evening, when we sat in our little casino, our only conversation, the war. When the glorious news of victory reached us, our jubilation knew no bounds. But in spite of this we felt an immense sadness – for we were not with our home armies!

The 15th of August arrived, and with it a communication of such enormity that we doubted the truth of what we read.

It ran as follows:

Extra Edition

"We consider it most important and necessary, with the object of maintaining a secure and lasting peace in the Far East, in accordance with the Anglo-Japanese Alliance Treaty, to take at the present moment every necessary measure to eliminate all causes likely to endanger peace.

"First, to withdraw the German warships at once from Japanese and Chinese waters, also armed ships of any description, and to dismantle those which cannot be withdrawn.

"Secondly, to surrender the whole Protectorate of Kiao-Chow forthwith – not later than by the 13th of September – to the Imperial Japanese Authorities without conditions or claims of indemnity, with the prospect of eventually returning the same to China.

"The Imperial Japanese Government announces at the same time that should it receive any but an unconditional acceptance from the Imperial German Government up to the 23rd of August 1914, to all the above-mentioned conditions, it will consider itself obliged to take such measures as the situation necessitates."

Our Governor had written below:

"It is a matter of course that we can never consent to surrender Kiao-Chow to Japan without drawing the sword. The frivolity of the Japanese demand admits but of one reply. But it implies that we must reckon on the opening of hostilities at the expiration of the date fixed. It will be a fight to the finish.

"Having regard to the gravity of the situation, we must proceed without further delay with the evacuation of women and children. Our Government will therefore place at their disposal a steamer prepared for the reception of 600 passengers, in order to convey them to Tientsin this day, Friday morning. It is urged that all who do not wish to stay here should take advantage of this opportunity, as well as of the trains, which are still running on the Shantung line.

"Kiao-Chow clears for action!"

We now knew exactly where we were. We had no illusions either as to the bitterness or the outcome of the coming fight. But never was work done in a higher or more indefatigable spirit. A titanic task was completed in these weeks. And, from the oldest officer to the youngest fifteen-year-old volunteer motorist, one and all combined in placing their knowledge, their ability, and endeavour at the service of their love for their country, in order to put Kiao-Chow in a state of defence.

I had experienced particularly bad luck. Three days after Müllerskowski's fall I rose in wonderful sunshine to my first important reconnaissance, and returned in a happy frame of mind to Kiao-Chow, after having explored the whole Protectorate for hundreds of miles.

I was at an altitude of 1500 metres, and in consequence of the atmospheric conditions the landing was a particularly difficult one. When I was about 100 metres over the place, and putting on full engine, with the object of flying round once more and landing to back, the engine started knocking and then stopped altogether. I only took a second to examine my altimeter, but it was sufficient to ascertain that the machine was no longer capable of landing on the aerodrome.

But I could veer neither to the right nor to the left. On the right hand there was the Polo Club and a deep ditch, on the left the hotel and villas.

I knew there was nothing more to be done, but I thought only of one thing: to keep the engine from harm.

In front of me lay a small wood, and I hoped to be able to negotiate it. I pulled at the altitude lever, but in the hot, thin air of the tropics the machine sagged heavily. I just managed to keep my head clear of the telegraph poles, then drew up my knees, pressed my feet unconsciously forward, and suddenly I felt a mighty shock, heard cracking and splintering noises, and collided heavily with the tank, after which all was silent. But when I looked around me, having miraculously escaped unhurt, I perceived my Taube with its nose in the ditch, its little tail high up in the air, and its wings and under-carriage forming a confused mass of broken wood, wires and canvas.

Oh, my poor little Taube! Would it had not happened exactly on the third day of the mobilization! I felt quite hopeless. Yet, without entirely losing courage, I carried the debris to the hangar. Luckily I had received some reserve propellers and planes from home.

My only hope was that the motor had escaped! I did not possess any spares, and it would have been impossible to procure them. I made my way towards the boxes in which the spares were kept, and first opened those which contained the planes. But, oh, horrors! A foul smell of decay was wafted into our faces, and, fearing the worst, we prised open the inner zinc lining.

The sight which met our eyes was perfectly horrible. The box was full of mouldy lumber. The covering of the planes had rotted. The wing ribs and the different wooden parts, which had been carefully packed, lay in a disorderly heap and were covered with a coat of mildew. It was a sad spectacle. We now opened the case in which were the propellers, where we found the same conditions. The five propellers had simply ceased to exist, and had shrunk to such an extent that they could no longer be of any use. It was a hard nut to crack!

But, without losing courage, my splendid rigger, Stüben, the chief mechanic, tackled the job, and the same afternoon I sat with Stüben, my two stokers, Frinks and Scholl, and eight Chinese from the dockyards, hard at work on the wings.

Thereafter I took the least damaged propeller to the wharf, and was helped out of my quandary, thanks to the excellent patternmaker K. who, with the Chinese, constructed a new propeller. This was a real masterpiece, for it was hewn out of seven thick oak planks which had been glued together with ordinary carpenter's glue. The Chinese used their axes, and fashioned a perfect propeller, copying a model which K. had set up for them. Though done by hand, their work showed the utmost care and precision.

It is this propeller I used for all my flights during the siege of Kiao-Chow.

But we had not remained idle in our sheds. We worked day and night with the utmost energy, and already, on the ninth day after my accident, my little Taube stood ready to run out on the aviation field at sunrise. It is not difficult, though, to understand that my expectations of a successful flight were not very high. My planes had been reconstructed from a mass of musty material, and we had to rig them the best we could, as we had no flat spaces. I have described the erection of the propeller which, by the way, made about a hundred revolutions less than it should have. Besides this, the conditions for flying on this particular aerodrome were so unfavourable that the choice lay between a clean start and an irremediable fall.

But I had no business to think of that. We were in the midst of war. I was the only aviator and had to carry on. And I had luck!

In order to lighten my machine I had scrapped every bit which I could do without. Therefore in the beginning my bird rose unwillingly to do my bidding, but soon I had regained full control over it. Hereafter I flew proudly, and dropped a message in front of the Governor's house: "Aircraft again in perfect order!"

I then began my long reconnoitring flights. I traversed the whole Protectorate, and flew hundreds of kilometres beyond it over the distant country, watching the ways of approach, and spying out the wild rocks of the coast, in order to see whether the enemy was near – or landing. These were the most beautiful expeditions of my life.

The air was so clear and transparent, the sky of such a pure azure, and the sun shone divinely and lovingly on the beautiful earth, on the cliffs and mountains, and the deep sea which hemmed the coast. My soul was athirst for beauty, and revelled in the marvellous sights of Nature for hours on end.

But I was not wholly without care. Already on my second flight I was able to ascertain that the glued grooves had split, and that by a miracle alone the propeller had not been torn asunder. It had, therefore, to be disconnected and freshly sized. This little performance had to be repeated after every flight. As soon as I returned, the propeller was taken off, I drove with my car to the wharves, there it got a fresh coat of mastic, was screwed under a press, and in the evening I fetched it, fixed it on the machine, and started afresh the next day.

But, as the propeller insisted on splitting regularly, I pasted the whole leading edge with canvas covering and sticking plaster, which helped a little towards holding it together.

At Kiao-Chow, over and above my regular duties, I was also in charge of the captive balloon section, which I jokingly called my "swollen-headed competitors!"

Before I left Berlin I had passed through a training course for dirigibles, learning to pilot airships, in addition to some practice with an observation balloon, and different practical exercises like mending balloon covers, etc.

The section, which was brand new, consisted of two huge balloons of 2000 cubic metres each, a balloon bag and all the necessary accessories for producing gas and for the service of the airships.

A petty officer, who had also had some experience with airships, was the only person, besides myself, who knew anything about it. After we had unpacked all the cases, we went very carefully about filling the balloons. And we were extremely proud when the first fat yellow sausage lay stoutly lashed to the ground. I, personally, fastened every line with my petty officer, and soon after this the yellow monster was swaying lightly under the blue canopy of the sky. We hauled it down, and I clambered alone into the gondola for the first ascent. On this occasion I very nearly started on my complicated voyage to Germany for, when the order "Let go!" was given, the rope, which had been measured out too generously, suddenly stiffened and got mixed up with the cable, whilst the balloon shot out perpendicularly 50 metres into the air. The thought that it was going to break away flashed through my mind. A violent jerk nearly threw me out of the gondola. But as the steel cable was also quite new it luckily held. So I was none the worse, except for having gained some fresh experience.

I then started drilling and instructing my crew, and soon the show was being run with the efficiency of old hands.

Our Governor expected great things of the observation balloon. It was hoped that it would be of great service in reconnoitring the approach of the enemy and the disposition of his artillery. These hopes were doomed to disappointment, and my fears that the erection of the balloons would serve no useful purpose proved only too justified.

Though I was able to send up the kite balloon to 1200 metres from the ground, we did not succeed in visualizing the range of hills which lay behind our fortified positions, thus observing the enemy's movements and, above all, the emplacement of his heavy siege artillery. And this would have been of capital importance to the defenders of Kiao-Chow.

The Protectorate of Kiao-Chow lies on a narrow strip of promontory which stretches out into the sea, with the town of Kiao-Chow framed on three sides by the sea and partitioned off from the mainland by a chain of mountains which has the form of a semicircle. They are the Moltke, Bismarck and Iltis Mountains. Our chief position nestled among their crannies, and at their foot lay the five infantry works with the barbed wire entanglements. Next came a wide valley, which was bisected by the river Haipo, and next a new range of hills, which also stretched from sea to sea and were doomed to bring disaster upon us. Behind them there was another broad valley surmounted by the wild rocky tips of the Lau-Hou-Schan, the Yung-Liu-Chui and the Lauchau.

It was most important for us to ascertain what was happening in the open country, as since the 27th of September we had been completely shut off behind our barbed wire. We were, above all, anxious to find out where the enemy kept his siege artillery and, as we had been disappointed in the reliability of our observation balloon, nothing remained but an occasional smart reconnaissance and – my aeroplane!

The days of August sped by in ceaseless labour. Kiao-Chow and its approaches became unrecognizable, and defensive positions for artillery were opened. To our sorrow the delightful little wood, which had been planted with so much care, the pride of Kiao-Chow, was felled by our axes to clear the zone of fire. How sad to destroy at one blow the loving work of "Kultur"!

The 23rd of August, the day on which the Japanese ultimatum expired, broke at last, and it is comprehensible that no answer was vouchsafed to the yellow Jap. The password was: "Go for them!" And this was our dearest wish.

I remember that, on the following morning, as I looked out from my balcony over the wide blue sea, I noticed at a distance of some nautical miles several black shadows which slowly moved to and fro. I was even able to distinguish torpedo boat destroyers through my telescope. Patzig, who came at a run to join my observations, also convinced himself of this. Of course – was it not the 24th? So the gang was blockading us! And the Japanese had actually dared to attack the German Empire!

The fight of a yellow race, abetted by a handful of Englishmen, against one German regiment on a war footing had begun.

Immediately on the expiration of the ultimatum a troop of one thousand men moved into the extreme outposts of the territory, in order to protect it as well as the roads of approach. This little detachment admirably fulfilled its task. It had to defend a tract of land which was 30 kilometres wide, and then another one of 10 kilometres, with quite insufficient artillery. A thousand men had to replace two army corps! They fought stubbornly and courageously, sometimes only able to oppose flying patrols to enemy battalions, retreating step by step before the fearful odds. Only on the 28th of September were they pushed back behind the principal retrenchments, which now definitely closed upon us until the end of the combat.

During the early days of the siege I must say that aeroplanes as well as aircraft generally were held in small esteem by the responsible authorities of the Kiao-Chow garrison. This, one must admit, was only natural, considering our luckless exhibitions. However, a swift change soon took place. One day I again flew over the south coast of the Shantung peninsula, on the look out for enemy ships or landing troops. The coast appeared deserted, and there was nothing to be seen. Much relieved that we were safe from that side at least, I flew home. Quite accidentally I went to Government House in the evening to see a comrade there. There I encountered by chance the head of the General Staff, who was in a tearing hurry as he had left an important conference at the Governor's in order to fetch a book.

He called out to me as he was passing: "Well, Plüschow, did you fly again?"

"Yes, sir," I said. "I have just returned. I searched the coast for enemy landing troops for several hours, but there is no sign of them."

I can still see the astounded expression on our Chief's face.

"What do you mean? Searched the coast? And only tell us now? Here we have been deliberating for the last two hours how we can ward off the large convoys which have been sighted by our scouts in the Dsin-Dsia-Kou Bay. And you have just come from there, and can produce such unimpeachable evidence? In you go to the Governor and report at once!"

The whole conference was now settled in a few words. The scouts' reports were, of course, inventions. But I was happy, for I had saved the reputation and the honour of aviation!

And now began my most difficult, but also most beautiful, flights.

I was soon to receive my baptism of fire. It was during the first days of September, on a Sunday, at an altitude of 1500 metres, far out over the territory, basking in the sunshine. I suddenly caught sight below of a fairly important detachment of Japanese, which greeted me with volleys of infantry and machine-gun fire. I returned home, exhibiting ten bullet holes in my planes. But, in future, I did not descend below 2000 metres, thus avoiding unnecessary risks to my engine and my propeller.

But the baptism of fire on land promptly followed.

Shortly afterwards, I motored to Shatsy-Kou, where we had advanced outposts. I stopped before the house without thought of danger. I was astonished to notice that all the officers and men were lying flat on the ground, along a stockade which was erected seawards. They waved their arms, which I naturally regarded as a greeting, answering them promptly in the same fashion.

I still sat in my car, when I heard a sibilant whistle sounding close to my head, followed by an ear-splitting crash not 10 feet away. A shell had exploded in the masonry of the house, and before I could recover from my surprise other projectiles followed the first.

I threw myself out of the car and took cover with the others. My brother officers were splitting with laughter for, however serious the situation, I must have looked a funny sight.

We then learned what had happened.

A Japanese destroyer flotilla lay in front and was trying to destroy Shatsy-Kou by her fire. We spent the next two hours under shell-fire, in our cramped and exposed position, without being able either to see or to move. At midday the Japs made a pause, probably in order to enjoy their dinner. While we examined the damage done to the house, the Chinese boys were already eagerly collecting shell-splinters. And, as we sat down for a moment to a cup of coffee, three small Chinks arrived with radiant faces, and planked three unexploded shells down in front of us. It would have made a fine mess if they had gone off then!

We started soon after on our return journey; but as we entered the first valley new shells exploded behind us – the bombardment was resumed.

A little later Shatsy-Kou had to be evacuated with the whole Protectorate, and on the 28th of September we retreated behind the principal retrenchments, and at the same time the first bombardment on a large scale was started from the sea.

"Some" noise!

In the early morning of that day I sat in my bath in the best of spirits, refreshing myself before a long flight, when I heard the most appalling noise. As our artillery had been active day and night, I did not pay much attention to this additional racket, but attributed it to the firing of our 28 centimetre howitzer of the Bismarck battery, which lay at the foot of my villa, and had so far kept silent to economize our ammunition.

I sent out my batman to see that my aeroplane was kept in readiness. But after a very few minutes he returned breathless and a little pale, and reported: "Sir, we must leave the villa at once; we are being bombarded by four big ships. One of the heavy shells has just landed near the sheds, but, thank God, the aeroplane is not damaged, and no one is hurt. But I burnt my fingers. I saw such a beautiful large splinter, and wanted to carry it away as a souvenir; it was *so* hot, but I got it, all the same!" And he beamingly showed me his singed pocket-handkerchief, which held the huge splinter of a 30 centimetre shell! But I was already out of my bath, and in two minutes had reached the aerodrome where, with combined efforts, we pushed my aeroplane into a more sheltered corner of the field. After that I ran to look at the bombardment from the shore commander's guardhouse.

The latter lay on a hill, from which one had an ideal view of Kiao-Chow. One could follow the flight of every shell, and from now onwards, whenever I was not flying, I sat up here during the next weeks, watching the fight.

The first bombardment of Kiao-Chow took place on the 28th of September, and was particularly impressive.

The crashing and bursting of the shells, with their accompanying roar, was accentuated by the echo from the surrounding mountains. Crash followed upon crash, and we had the impression that the whole of Kiao-Chow was being turned into a heap of ruins. It was a weird feeling, but we soon got used to it. One is completely helpless in the face of exploding shells, and can but wait until all is over, whilst hoping that one may be mercifully far away from the spot on which they fall.

How despicable the English must have felt during this bombardment and those that followed!

The enemy ships stood so far out that our guns could not reach them. Therefore, they were quite safe. In the van steamed three Japanese battleships, and under Japanese command, at the rear, the English battleship *Triumph*.

I wonder whether the English felt proud of their rôle as executioners?

Thank God, the damage caused by the bombardment was not of much consequence, and from then on we awaited their cannonading with the greatest calm.

In the evening I witnessed a particularly sad performance. Our gunboats, *Cormoran*, *Iltis* and *Luchs*, were sunk by us after they had been dismantled.

It was a tragic sight. The three ships were fastened together and towed by a steamer into deep water and there blown up and burnt. It seemed as if the three ships knew that they were being dragged to their doom. They looked infinitely sad and helpless, with their bare masts sticking up heavenwards, and their frames writhed in the fire, as if they were unwilling to turn into ashes, until the waves swept over them and put an end to their torment. Our sailors' hearts were wrung with pity. These three were followed by *Lauting* and

Taku, and, shortly before our surrender, by the little *Jaguar* and the Austrian cruiser, *Kaiserin Elisabeth*, after these two ships had rendered us invaluable service. Their work fills one of the most glorious pages in the history of the fight and death of Kiao-Chow.

Chapter Four

Some Japanese Jokes

We were greatly puzzled by the activity of the Japanese besieging army. After the first bombardment we all thought that the Japanese would try to carry the fortress by assault, as they could not fail to know how weak we were, and that but a single wire entanglement stood between them and us.

The wildest rumours were circulated in our midst: "The Japanese dare not attack us, as things are going so well for us in Europe!" or "The Americans are sending their fleet to our assistance, and will force the Japs to retire!" And then again, "The Japs only want to starve us out; they want Kiao-Chow to fall into their hands with as little damage as possible!"

But we never got beyond mere conjectures. Quietly and systematically, and without our being able to prevent them, the Japanese landed their troops, constructed roads and railways, brought up heavy artillery and ammunition, entrenched themselves before our entanglements and slowly worked towards our defence-line.

I now started on. my principal job – to reconnoitre the position of the enemy's heavy batteries.

Every day, whenever the weather permitted – and the propeller! – in the early dawn, as soon as it was light, I started on my travels into the unknown. And when the sun rose I hung like a silver speck high up in the ether, circling for hours round the enemy's positions, and overlooking the whole of our beloved Protectorate invaded by an impudent enemy, who meant to corner and destroy us.

My work was hard, but I enjoyed it, and it was crowned with success, and the enemy's unceasing efforts to shoot me down convinced me that I *was* successful.

As I mentioned before, I was now the only aviator at Kiao-Chow – "the Master-Bird of Kiao-Chow", as the Chinese called me. Also I had but a single Taube at my disposal. I had to be careful and take no unnecessary risks, otherwise there would have been an end to my job.

This was the way I carried out my reconnoitring.

As soon as I was flying right over the enemy I throttled my engine in such a fashion that it kept the altitude of its own accord. I then hung my map on the stick, took a pencil and a notebook, and observed what was happening below through the space between the planes and the tail. I let go the stick, and steered solely with my feet.

I then circled round a position until I had thoroughly mastered its details, made a sketch of them, and entered them in my notebook. I soon acquired such proficiency that I was able to write and draw uninterruptedly for an hour or two. When I felt the back of my neck getting stiff, I turned round and looked down on the other side. I did this until I was satisfied with my notes, and sometimes I was so carried away by my work that I had to be warned by a glance at my petrol recorder that it was high time I went home.

I always returned the same way. I flew round the wharves and the town in proud circles, and when I reached my aerodrome I shut off the engine and shot down to earth in a steep, gliding flight, which landed me safe and sound in four minutes. For it was necessary to be quick. Infantry and machine gun fire were continuously directed at my aeroplane while it flew over the enemy's positions; when this proved of no avail, the enemy used shrapnel, and this was most objectionable.

The Japanese always had new surprises in store for me. One day, for instance – a day of blue sky and glorious sunshine – as I was returning from a reconnaissance and about to land, I saw a great number of fleecy white clouds, which looked perfectly delightful seen from above, hovering over my aerodrome at an altitude of about 300 metres.

But I soon noticed that the Japanese were trying on one of their little jokes, for these pretty cloudlets were caused by the firing of 10½ centimetre shrapnels!

There was nothing to be done but to grind one's teeth and fight one's way through. Four minutes later my machine dropped from an altitude of 2000 metres, and I pushed it as quickly as I could under a shed, whose roof was protected by earth.

I had now to resort to ruse.

Sometimes, when still hovering over the enemy camp, I suddenly shut off my engine and swooped down perpendicularly on to a corner of my aerodrome, so that the Japs were convinced that they had winged me. By the time they recovered from their surprise I was already pushing my machine into safety, their shrapnel bursting much too late.

But, as I tirelessly returned, the Japanese retaliated by posting two of their 10½ centimetre batteries so far behind and so much on the side that their shrapnel easily reached me whilst I was circling over their heads. It was very unpleasant, and my fate would often have been sealed but for my nimbleness in taking a sharp turn and thus evading a hit.

The shrapnels then burst so near that in spite of the noise of the engine I could hear the ugly bark of the explosion and feel the violent air pressure that sent my aeroplane 'rolling like an old barge at sea, which made observation extremely difficult.

I must say that each time I landed safely I felt an overwhelming pride and satisfaction in my achievement, and halloed joyously with the full power of my lungs.

After hours of the greatest exertion and danger, I again felt solid earth under my feet, and in spite of guns and shrapnel.

As soon as I touched ground my four helpers came on the run, fearless of danger from the hail of shrapnel, and helped me to stow away my machine. My faithful dog, Husdent, jumped around them, barking joyously.

And whilst the four were busy getting, my aeroplane ready for the next flight, I already sat at the steering-wheel of my car, all my maps and reports in my pocket, with Husdent at my side, and again raced along the road under shrapnel fire to Government House, where my reports were being eagerly awaited.

I believe anybody will sympathize with my joy and pride when I was allowed to present my drawings and observations. For on some days I had been able to discover as many as five or six enemy batteries, and often my observations filled four pages of the report forms.

The warm handshake with which the Governor and the Head of the Staff thanked me for my work was reward enough.

And whilst I drove homewards, in order to lunch and take a much needed rest, I already heard the thundering of our guns as they hurtled their iron hailstones into the positions of the enemy just discovered by me.

Chapter Five

My War Ruse

How sad and desolate it now looked in my little house!

Immediately at the beginning of the siege, my good Patzig was obliged to leave me and to rejoin his 21 centimetre battery commander. He had only luxuriated for four weeks in the possession of our beautiful little home, and now he sat in his redoubt and fulfilled his duty until he had fired his last shell and the Japanese, with their heavy howitzers, had levelled to the ground the whole of his battery.

As soon as the first shot was fired, my Chinese cook, Moritz, faithlessly left me in the lurch, and one evening I found that also Fritz, Max and August had vanished without trace.

After a few days a new Chinese cook – Wilhelm – appeared on the scene, and recounted with emphatic gestures:

"Kind Master, me plenty good cook; me no lun away like bad fellow Molitz; me havee no fear; me makee plenty good chau-chau."

I believed him, promised to give him five dollars and more. Things went fairly well, until one day the first enemy shells burst close to my house, and Herr Wilhelm as promptly disappeared as his predecessors.

I now sat alone in my deserted home with my faithful batman, Dorsch. We were the only inhabitants of the whole villa quarter of Iltis Bay.

Not exactly a safe or pleasant spot, for the villas were built on the hill which carried our chief batteries, and the enemy shells which whizzed past them landed straight in our midst. But we were very cautious. That is to say, we left our top floor and settled down comfortably and safely on the ground floor. As a further precaution we placed our beds in a corner, in such a way that they were far from a window, and thus we secured sufficient immunity. It was, however, lucky that no heavy shell challenged this position.

But I did not remain for long in sole control of the air.

On the forenoon of the 5th of September, under an overcast sky, with low-hanging clouds, we suddenly heard the purring of a motor, and I ran home to see what had happened. I was hardly there when an immense biplane shot into sight close over our heads. I was speechless, and peered dazedly at the apparition. Soon, however, the first explosions rent the air, and I now perceived the round red balls under the planes.

It was a Jap!

I must say that I felt rather queer on beholding my huge enemy colleague floating so near us in the sky. A bright outlook for the future!

Kiao-Chow regarded the advent of the enemy airman as a most disagreeable surprise, for no one had expected that the Japs would be equipped with aircraft.

On the whole, they eventually produced eight aeroplanes, amongst them four gigantic seaplanes, for whose possession I heartily envied the Japs. How often in the ensuing weeks did I gaze longingly at them, as they circled round the town, and wish for one!

The Japs flew well and with extraordinary pluck. It is lucky, however, that their bomb-dropping was not on a par with it, otherwise it would have been a bad look out for us. The Japanese bombs were heavy, of recent construction, and most destructive.

The enemy seaplanes also had a tremendous advantage over us. They were able to take off at a great distance, without consideration of the wind, with as much space for turning out as they could wish for; and when they had ascended with the greatest security to the altitude of 3000 metres they swooped down upon us, and simply jeered at our shrapnels and machine-guns.

One of the chief aims of the enemy was to destroy my hangar. Soon matters became so unpleasant for my aerodrome that one fine day I decided that it was time to stop my enemy colleagues' little game.

My real shed lay at the northern end of the ground; it made a splendid target, and the Japanese knew its location by heart. I now built unobtrusively a new shed on the opposite side, close to a mountain slope, covering it with clods of earth and grass, so that nothing of it could be noticed from above. We then proceeded with deep cunning and malice to the erection of a bogus aeroplane, with the help of planks, sailing canvas and tin. From above it looked exactly like my Taube. And after that, the moment an enemy aviator was in sight, we played a little comedy.

On some days the doors of my old shed were wide open, and my imitation Taube sprawled in front of it on the beautiful green grass. On others the shed was closed and nothing was to be seen. Another day my sham machine sat in a different place, where it could be spotted at once. Now the enemy aviators arrived and dropped bombs and bombs in their endeavours to hit the innocent bird. Whilst this was going on we sat in the real aeroplane, well protected by our roof, holding our sides with laughter as we saw the bombs seeking their bogus victim.

Once when we had been specially deluged with them, I picked out a fine splinter from a Japanese aviation bomb, affixed my visiting card to it and wrote:

"Kindest greetings to the enemy colleagues! Why do you shy at us with such hard objects? If you aren't careful you will end by hurting us! It isn't done."

I took this letter on my next flight and dropped it in front of the Japanese seaplane station.

But this was only to announce my visit.

In the meantime one of our men had been preparing bombs for me. Simply marvellous specimens! Huge tin boxes of 4 lb. each, on which could be read in big letters: "Sietas, Plambeck & Co., best Java coffee". They were filled with dynamite, horseshoe nails and scrap iron, a lead spar fixed to the bottom and a fuse at the top. It was exploded by a sharp iron point which hit the percussion-cap of a cartridge. All these things seemed pretty uncanny to me, and I handled them with the greatest caution – always happy when I had done with them. But they never caused much damage. Once I hit a torpedo boat, and even then it did not explode; on several occasions I just missed a convoy. And once I learned through Japanese reports that I had dropped a bomb into the midst of a Japanese marching column and sent thirty yellow ones to the nether regions!

I soon got over the first pleasant emotion of bombing. My time was fully occupied apart from it, and the results did not justify the time I lost.

I often met my enemy colleagues in the air. I did not hanker for these meetings, for I could do little with my slow, laboriously climbing Taube against the huge biplanes which carried a crew of three men. Above all, I dared not forget that my chief object was reconnoitring, and after that to bring back my machine to Kiao-Chow in good condition.

Once I was busily engaged on my observations, when my aeroplane began to pitch and toss. I thought this was due to bumps in the air, caused by the many steep and rugged mountains of this country which made flying extraordinarily difficult. Without even looking up, I went on taking observations, only grasping the control-lever with one hand in order to keep the aeroplane steady.

After my return I was informed, to my great surprise, that an enemy plane had flown so closely on top of me that they thought I should be shot down.

Next time I was more careful. And on sighting one of my enemy colleagues I followed and shot him down with my Parabellum pistol, after firing thirty times.

A short time afterwards I nearly shared his fate. I was only at an altitude of 1700 metres, and in spite of the greatest efforts I could not get any higher. I was just above the enemy seaplane station as one of the great biplanes started. I now carried out my reconnaissance, thinking to myself: "Well, he can bestir himself until he gets up as high as I!"

But after forty minutes, when I looked on my left over the plane, I saw the enemy already gaining on me at a distance of only a few thousand metres. This meant to be on guard and climb higher. But my Taube simply refused to budge, and I could not gain another yard. A quarter of an hour only elapsed before the other chap had outdistanced me, and was coming diagonally across my trail, trying to cut me off from the road to Kiao-Chow.

It was now a matter for betting who would first reach Kiao-Chow, but I won the race. When I returned to my aerodrome I simply dived down, and no sooner did I reach the ground than bombs were bursting all around us.

It is extraordinary how they sometimes find their mark!

Strict orders had been given at Kiao-Chow that everybody should make for cover as soon as an enemy airman was sighted. We had only two casualties – a non-commissioned officer and a Chinese. And that was quite marvellous enough. On my aerodrome I had about one hundred coolies, and they always sped to safety. One day, however, a native remained standing in the middle of the ground, all on his lonesome, staring at the large bird. Bang! A bomb hurtled through the air and exploded but a few paces away. The poor devil was badly hit. To have really bad luck there is no easier way than to be on the spot where shells and other heavy missiles are flying about.

Chapter Six

Hurrah!

How did things look at Kiao-Chow in the meantime? The bombardment from the sea had become a daily occurrence, and soon the land batteries added their boom to the hellish discord. There was no longer any safety apart from the bomb proof redoubts and localities. The firing became heavier and heavier, and on some days from the sea alone several hundred 30 centimetre, half naval shells were shot into little Kiao-Chow.

On the 14th of October our naval fortifications of Hu-Chuin-Huk were directly under fire. The enemy ships were far out at sea, and after the second volley the little outpost was submerged beneath a deluge of heavy shells. Now volley followed volley. The whole fortifications disappeared from sight behind the columns of water, flames and smoke, and the rumbling and crashing of the bursting shells set the earth a-tremble.

As usual, I stood that morning on the coast commander's look out, about 1000 metres from the fort, and so witnessed this terrifying spectacle at first hand.

Sometimes the yard long shell splinters flew whirring and hissing weirdly over our heads, without our paying any attention to them, as we were so engrossed by what we saw, which was so stupendous that no words could fittingly describe it.

We thought with deep sorrow of the brave garrison and of their sure destruction; but suddenly, in the midst of the heaviest fire, our old 24 centimetre gun fired one shot, and our field-glasses were immediately fixed on the enemy ships.

Suddenly a joyful and triumphant "Hurrah!" burst from our lips, for one of our explosive shells had hit the English warship *Triumph* plumb in the middle of her deck. *Triumph* veered at once and ran away for all she was worth, and when our second shell sped after her a little later it was only able to hit the water about 50 metres from her stern.

Triumph steamed away after a few signals, which she exchanged with the Japanese flagship, and went off to Yokohama for repairs.

The three Japanese ships continued their bombardment – now at a more respectful distance – so that it was useless to fire any longer with our old guns, which could not travel half as far.

At midday the bombardment ceased at last, the enemy being justified by that time in assuming that the fort was destroyed and all its inmates killed.

The staff of the coast commander at once hurried to Fort Hu-Chuin-Huk; and I also followed in my motor-car.

Still under the impression of the terrible spectacle of the bombardment, we were most surprised on our arrival to see the whole garrison merrily tearing round, collecting splinters and admiring the huge craters which the enemy shells had dug in the ground.

What luck! Not a man wounded, not a gun injured, not a hit on the bomb proof rooms!

The whole result of the heavy bombardment amounted to a broken biscuit tin and a soldier's shirt, which was hanging out to dry, and was torn to shreds! It was strange to think that 51 and 30½ centimetre guns were used to such purpose!

A heavy shell had passed clean through the thin steel turrets, and lay peacefully near the gun on the iron plates!

Now we learned the secret of our lucky hit – our guns had in reality only a carrying range of 160–100. But the gunners had with infinite pains succeeded in raising the gun several sixteenths of a degree higher, and so it carried 200 to 300 metres farther.

Having loaded the breech at its highest angle, the brave gunners and their gallant battery commander, Oberleutnant Hasshagen, had quietly stuck to their guns under the heaviest shell fire, until at last one of the ships came within hitting distance. And the best of it was that it hit the right target! It is a pity that the *Triumph* ran away so quickly, otherwise she would not have escaped her fate on that day. But, for all that, it overtook her a little later.

What we could not achieve was accomplished in the spring of 1915 by our friend Hersing, when he, with his U-boat, sent this same *Triumph* to the bottom of the sea in the Dardanelles, thus avenging the garrison of Kiao-Chow. We owe him a debt of gratitude for this service.

Ties of sincere friendship bound me to the officers and the garrison of Fort Hu-Chuin-Huk.

I did not really belong to them, for in the first place my aerodrome lay close to the fort, and, in the second, they regularly watched my start and, above all, my endeavours to get clear of their guns. And more than once the men stood ready to jump into the sea to save me, for they thought I was falling into the water with my machine.

But as often as I was a guest of the remarkable Commander of the Fort, Kapitanleutnant Kopp, we painted our triumphant return to Germany after the war in the most glowing colours, and had of course decided that I should march in with the garrison of Fort Hu-Chuin-Huk.

On the 17th of October, late in the evening, a group of officers assembled on the coast commander's stand and waited in breathless suspense for her commander, Kapitanleutnant Brunner, to run the blockade with his torpedo boat destroyer S90.

Two evenings before he had been out in a gallant endeavour to lay mines on the track of the Japanese ships. Today he was going to fulfil his last and most difficult task – to break through the line of the enemy torpedo boat destroyers and attack one of the enemy ships. It was a clear night, and there would be no moon after ten. The time came. Ten struck, then 10.30 – the tension became unbearable. Nothing could be seen of S90. Suddenly – it was eleven – we perceived a narrow, grey shadow which carefully moved on the water under the Pearl Mountains. And soon our sharp sailors' eyes recognized the shape of the torpedo boat. "Good luck to your brave men!" Our hearts accompanied them with our warmest wishes. The boat disappeared from our sight, and soon the dangerous moment was at hand when they would have to break through the enemy lines. Our eyes were glued in fascination on the open sea, expecting the flashing of the searchlights and the thunder of the guns at any moment.

But all was silence.

It was midnight. Another half-hour sped by – we breathed more easily, for the enemy was still in ignorance of the coming attack. By this time our boat must have reached the bulk of the fleet. The minutes turned into hours. No one spoke.

Suddenly at 1 a.m., far away towards the south on the open sea, a huge fire-column, and then from all sides the lurid, groping fingers of the searchlights and a distant muttering and vibrating.

Hurrah! That was the work of S90. And already at 1.30 we received the following wireless:

"Have attacked enemy cruisers with three torpedoes, registered three hits. Cruiser blew up at once. Am hunted by torpedo boat destroyers, return Kiao-Chow cut off, trying escape south and, if necessary, shall explode boat.

Brunner.

This wire is sufficient praise for Commander, officers and crew.

A few weeks later, without premonition, I met the S90 at Nanking – but that is another story.

Chapter Seven

The Last Day

The siege progressed according to plan. The Japanese dug themselves in ever closer; they brought up more and more heavy guns, and on several occasions large bodies of Japanese infantry made night attacks on our infantry positions – to be, however, repulsed each time. After this they subjected the latter and the wire entanglements in front of them to continuous fire, which ceased neither by night nor by day. Our guns, too, were never silent, but unfortunately we had to go slow on account of our remaining ammunition. The extraordinary length of the siege, the never ceasing artillery fire, and the terrible tension under which we lived, began to tell on us. My own nerves were getting out of hand.

I could no longer force myself to eat, and sleep had become impossible. When I shut my eyes at night I immediately saw my map, and below me the Protectorate with its enemy trenches and positions. My head swam, and my ears ached from the whirl of the propeller, and I could hear, over and over again, the words of the Chief of Staff:

"Never forget, Plüschow, that you are now of more value to Kiao-Chow than our daily bread. Don't fail to return and keep the machine going! And don't forget that our shells are few, and that we use them according to your indications. Remember your responsibilities!"

God knows I was in no danger of forgetting them. I had no other thought but the enemy positions in my mind, visualizing time and again the fortifications over which I had flown, trying to remember whether I had actually seen what I had reported, and figuring out whether the few shells which we still possessed had not been squandered at my instigation.

When I had racked my brain fruitlessly for hours I sometimes fell asleep about three in the morning, tired out in body and soul. But no sooner had I dropped off than duty called, and my mechanic stood at my bedside to report that my machine was ready for another flight. This meant prompt action, and I was soon standing next to my Taube, testing all her parts.

Sometimes I felt queer and rather jumpy; but as soon as I was settled in my pilot's seat and held the throttle in my hand, after nodding to my helpers, I had only one thought, and that was to carry out my task with iron determination and calmness. And when I had got over the start, and safely reached an altitude of a few hundred metres, I felt quite at ease again.

One circumstance depressed me particularly – the absolute loneliness, the eternal solitude of my flights. If I had only had a comrade with whom I might have exchanged occasional signs, it would have helped me enormously. And another cause for despondency was the impossibility of any flights for several days on end, owing to the rain or to my faulty propeller. And when I started again I found so many changes in the enemy's positions that I very nearly gave way to despair. What could I do in the face of this tangle of trenches, zigzags and new positions? Often the map dropped from my nerveless fingers. But this was not a lasting phase.

I pulled myself together, picked up my pencil and gazed downwards. And soon I had no eyes for anything happening round me – my entire attention was focused on the enemy and my notes.

The 27th of October was a fête day for us. The following telegram was received from His Majesty the Kaiser:

"Both I and the whole German nation look with pride on the
heroes of Kiao-Chow, who carry out their duty faithful to the
word of their Governor. Rest assured of My gratitude."

There was hardly anyone in Kiao-Chow whose heart did not beat
the faster for this praise. Our supreme War Lord, who had so much
heavy work on hand at home, did not forget his faithful little band
in the Far East. Each of us swore to do his duty to the end, in order
to please his Kaiser.

Soon the 31st of October – the Mikado's birthday – was upon
us. We had ascertained, through our scouts, that the Japanese had
fixed on that day for the capture of Kiao-Chow. It is impossible to
describe it.

The Japs had planted all their land batteries in readiness for the
night and at 6 a.m., on the 31st of October 1914, the bombardment
started from land and sea.

Their first hits exploded the petrol tanks, and a thick, huge
column of smoke reared skywards like an ominous signal of revenge.
The Japanese were shooting from the land with heavy 20 centimetre
shells, and the ships had trained their heaviest guns on to us. The
whizzing of the descending howitzer shells, the whistling and the
exploding of the grenades and their detonations on bursting, the
barking of shrapnel, and the roar of our own guns resulted in a din
as though hell itself had been let loose.

The outworks and the whole surrounding country were also heavily
damaged; hilltops were levelled, deep craters opened in the ground.

By the evening we experienced a slackening of the enemy's fire.
He was convinced, and so were we, that all our defences had been
razed, for they looked like a mass of ruins. But when our gallant
lads in blue hurried to their guns, to dig them out of the mass of

earth and stone, they found nearly all the batteries comparatively undamaged.

Suddenly in the dead of night, when we were able to note the formation of the storming columns, from every cannon's mouth issued a stream of fire, which must have caused endless casualties to the Japanese.

There was no attack, as had been planned, and the next day the enemy artillery directed a half-hearted bombardment on us. At the same time it was vigorous enough to register fifty successful hits on our small fort of Hu-Chuin-Huk.

The Japanese profited by the experience of that night. Eight terrible days and nights followed, for their artillery thundered without a break.

It might well have been assumed that not one of us could have escaped this ghastly, thunderous fire; but, as if by a miracle, we had very few casualties. The Japanese artillery shot with great precision, which is not surprising, as many of their artillery officers had been trained at our gunnery school at Juteborg. But their ammunition was rotten. And that proved our salvation.

They never once succeeded in penetrating any of our redoubts or bomb proof localities.

To this, as well as to their blank shooting, we owe our insignificant losses.

I would like to point out to the cavillers in Germany, who grumbled that our fight for Kiao-Chow could not have been serious if we suffered comparatively so little, that we held but one single line of defence, composed of five infantry works, a parapet and a miserable wire entanglement. This line was 6000 metres long and held by 3000 men. We had neither a second line nor a second position and, above all, no men to spare for their defence, for our whole garrison comprised but 4000 men.

When after a week of heavy continuous artillery fire our wire entanglements and parapet had been shot to pieces, it was an easy job for the 30,000 Japanese – whom we had held at bay for weeks – to rush through and force the surrender of Kiao-Chow.

In the early days of November we prepared for the end. On the 1st, our loyal ally, the Austrian cruiser *Kaiserin Elisabeth*, was blown up by her gallant crew after she had fired her last shot. A few days later she was followed by our last ship, the brave little gunboat Jaguar.

Our deck and crane followed, and then came the turn of our wharves.

We no longer had much help from our guns. A few were out of action, others had been destroyed by enemy artillery, the greater number we blew up ourselves.

On the 5th of November 1914 I myself was forced to undertake the destruction of my biplane. I had succeeded, assisted by an Austrian ex-aviator, Leutnant Clobuczar, in the construction of a wonderful, large two-seater hydroplane. It lay in readiness, and it had been my intention to reconnoitre with it, as it was no longer possible to use our aviation field, which was only 4000 to 5000 metres distant, but held under the steady fire of the enemy.

Nothing was to come of my biplane, and all our labour was in vain, for that afternoon our Chief summoned me and said:

"We are expecting the Japanese main attack at any hour now. See that you leave the fortress by aeroplane, though I fear the Japs will give you no time to do so. And now, God speed you, and may you come through safely. I thank you for the work you did for Kiao-Chow!"

He gave me his hand. I said, standing at attention:

"I report myself obediently as leaving the fortress!"

And with this I was dismissed.

I took leave of my superior officers and of my comrades, and was entrusted with a large bundle of private correspondence. Then I went back to my villa for the last time, and said good-bye to my rooms and to the many objects to which I had become attached. I opened my stable door, freed my little horse and my chickens, and went down to my aeroplane to prepare it for its last flight. After that I sat poring over my map, learning it by heart, and making my calculations.

At night I went up to the hill-top, where my friend, Oberleutnant Aye, had been holding out for weeks with his small battery under most severe shell-fire. From there one had a magnificent view of Kiao-Chow and its surroundings. I sat for some time on the highest peak, fascinated by the panorama at my feet. Below us a sea of fire, with flashes of lightning from the guns thundering across space, and the yellow rifle and machine gun fire was like a golden thread stretched from sea to sea. Right over my head screamed, swished and whistled thousands of shells, sweeping closely over the hill top, bent on reaching their targets. Behind me our heavy howitzers roared their last message and in the distance, from the farthest southern point of Kiao-Chow, the 29 centimetre guns of Fort Hstanniwa poured out their swan song.

Harrowed to the depths of my soul, I returned to Aye, and after taking a hearty leave of him, carrying with me all his good wishes for my venture, I left him, after shaking him warmly by the hand.

I was the last officer in Kiao-Chau to do so, for he fell a few hours later in the heroic but unequal fight against the Japanese, he and his gallant little band preferring death to surrender. A truly shining example of noble heroism.

I spent the remaining hours with my four brave helpers, waiting in readiness near my machine so as to be able to carry out my orders at a moment's notice should the Japanese break through.

On the 6th of November 1914, in the early dawn, with the moon still shining, my aeroplane stood clear for the start, and my propeller gaily hummed its morning hymn.

There was no more time to lose. The aviation field had become extremely uncomfortable through the continuous shell and shrapnel fire.

Once more I examined my machine, shook hands with my men, stroked the head of my faithful dog, then I opened the throttle and my Taube shot like an arrow into the night.

Suddenly, as I was just about 30 metres above the centre of the aerodrome, my machine received a fearful jar, and I was only able to prevent her crashing downwards by putting forth all my strength. An enemy grenade had just burst, and the air-pressure caused by the detonation nearly sent me to the ground. But, thank goodness, a big hole in my left plane caused by a shell-splinter was the only damage.

The usual hail of shrapnel followed – my last farewells from the Japs and their English allies.

When I was high enough I turned round once more to look at our dear little Kiao-Chow, which had suffered and was still to suffer so much. Our beloved second country – Paradise on earth.

Two lines of fire, facing each other, were clearly distinguishable, and the faint roar of guns could be heard – sure forerunners of renewed attack and desperate defence.

Would we be able to ward it off for the third time? I waved my hand towards Kiao-Chow! Farewell, my faithful comrades, fighting down there!

This leave taking was infinitely bitter, and I struggled for composure. I flung my machine round with a swift wrench, and steered it towards Cape Taschke.

When the sun rose in all its glory, I was already floating in the blue ether, high over the wild southern mountain peaks.

I had run the blockade in true modern fashion.

Chapter Eight

In the Slime of the Chinese Rice-Field

The enemy fleet lay at anchor behind the Pearl Mountains. I could not resist the temptation, and flew round them once again. Then I wended my way farther and farther towards South China, an unknown land and an uncertain fate. I passed over rugged mountains, over rivers and wide plains, sometimes crossing the open sea, then again high above towns and villages.

I guided myself by map and compass, and at 8 a.m. I had already put 250 kilometres behind me, and reached my destination – Hai-Dschou, in the province of Kiangsu.

I peered into the plain below in search of a suitable landing-place; but my prospects were not too promising.

The torrential rains of the past weeks had turned the ground into a veritable swamp. The only dry spots were covered with houses or Chinese burial-mounds. Finally I discovered a small field, 200 metres long and 20 metres wide, which was bounded by deep ditches and high walls on two sides, and by the river on the others.

Landing was confoundedly difficult, but there was no help for it, for I could not stay up for ever. Besides, I was in China, not in Germany, and could count myself lucky to have found this spot at all.

I descended in wide curves. And after a steep spiral, during which the machine sagged heavily in consequence of the depression in the atmosphere, I landed in the middle of the swampy rice field at 8.45 a.m.

The clay was so soft and sticky that the aeroplane sank into the mud and the wheels were held fast; my machine landed on her nose, nearly turning turtle at the last moment. The propeller shivered into fragments, but luckily I escaped without hurt.

The silence which reigned struck me as uncanny after the incessant crash and turmoil of war of the last weeks. My little Taube rested calmly and peacefully in the bright sunshine, with her little tail up and her nose embedded in the mud. I could distinguish a crowd of Chinese in the distance – men, women and swarms of children – pressing forward in awed wonder. They, together with all the other Chinese over whose land I had flown, could not account for my presence, for I was the first aviator they had ever seen, and they were all convinced that I was an Evil Spirit bent on their destruction. So when I clambered out of my machine and tried to signal to them, there was no holding them. They all fled, howling and screaming, the men first, leaving the children who dropped behind as peace offerings to the devil. I do not think my appearance could have caused greater consternation in darkest Africa.

With prompt decision I ran after them, hauling three or four of them by their pigtails to the machine, so as to convince, them that the big bird was harmless.

This helped after a little, and when I presented them with some gold pieces they averred that by a lucky chance they were in the presence of a Good Spirit; therefore, they willingly helped to place the aeroplane in a horizontal position once more. When the others saw this, they gathered round in such crowds that I was surprised the machine was not crushed.

How the Chinese marvelled! How they touched and examined everything! How they laughed and chattered!

Only those who know the Chinese and their childlike disposition can gauge the amusing situation in which I found myself.

I sat in my pilot's seat, over the tin box containing the secret papers, with a Mauser pistol close to my hand, surrounded by a horde of

Nature's children, whom it was impossible to get rid of, though I repeatedly made the attempt. The creatures merely grinned joyously and made fun of me.

I was at last freed from this predicament by a "Good morning, sir," boomed into my ear. A gentleman, who introduced himself as Dr. Morgan of the American Mission, stood before me. We greeted each other warmly, and I informed Dr. Morgan of what had happened, and asked him to use his knowledge of the Chinese language, which he spoke fluently, to help me. I soon saw that I was in good hands.

My huge Chinese passport, which I had brought with me from Kiao-Chow, was immediately sent to the Mandarin; an hour later a detachment of forty soldiers arrived from the barracks situated a short distance off, to keep guard over my machine.

I gladly accepted Dr. Morgan's invitation to breakfast and, laden with all the movable objects in my aeroplane, I set off with him to the Mission.

I was welcomed most charmingly, and made the acquaintance of Mrs. Morgan, also of Mrs. Rice, the wife of the American missionary, and of a Mr. G., who all took the warmest interest in me.

I had just sat down to breakfast when a Chinese officer appeared, with the announcement that a guard of honour, consisting of a company of soldiers, had been placed before the house, and that he was under orders from his Mandarin to ascertain my wishes, and how I was. The Mandarin himself, however, would call on me in half an hour.

I was delighted at so much courtesy.

After another ten minutes new visitors arrived; this time the civic authorities of Hai-Dschou, who desired to greet me in person.

The situation was unique. I sat in the midst of these venerable old Chinese, having exchanged numerous bows and obeisances.

The conversation soon become animated, Dr. Morgan acting as interpreter.

There was no end to their questions: Whence did I come? How were things in Kiao-Chow? Was it really true that I had come through the air? How long had I taken for my flight? What magic had I used to be able to fly? It was hardly possible to answer all their posers, and, though our interpreter took infinite trouble, I am sure that the Sons of Heaven were not much the wiser.

Soon there was a slight break.

While we sat talking, visitors were announced for the lady of the house, and ten or twelve delightful little Chinese women, swathed in wonderful silken garments and trousers, tripped past us. Two or three of them lingered near the door of the room in which we men were seated, and stared at us in awed fascination with big, round eyes and small, half opened mouths. Mrs. Morgan called to them from the adjoining room, and they gave a frightened start and ran away. I only learnt the reason for their strange conduct later. It seems that it is a social faux pas for a Chinese woman of gentle birth to offend a male visitor by her curious glances.

The three sinners received a severe reprimand. I must admit I did not care for this custom, for I should have liked a good look at the elegant little ladies.

My hostess confided to me that she, too, had been pestered by questions from her guests. Above all, they wished to know who this Evil Spirit was which had threatened their town, yelling and growling. When they were informed that it was a mere man who came from Kiao-Chow, they laughed and declared that they were not fools enough to believe that!

Mrs. Morgan assured me laughingly that everything that might happen to go wrong in the next two years, such as bad harvests, miscarriages, mishaps of any description, would be put down to my account, and prove of invaluable service to the medicine men.

The Mandarin arrived about eleven, preceded by an uproar of tom-toms, drums and whistles. He advanced with great dignity, an imposing figure of rotund proportions, with a carefully shaven head, clad in magnificent silken garments. Our salutations were extremely formal, and the deep bows to the ground seemed endless.

The Mandarin inquired thoughtfully after my health and wishes, and assured me of his aid and protection. He took leave with the same ceremony.

As soon as I had returned this official visit, and had been invited to sup with the Mandarin, I proceeded to dismantle my aeroplane.

But this was more easily said than done. I only possessed a spanner, and had now to hunt for tools. Moreover, I was in China, and in a part of the country where the last thousand years had brought no changes. Wrenches or screwdrivers were unknown quantities.

At length I discovered an axe in the American Mission, and a miserable object that looked like a saw.

I set to work with these implements, and, as I wished at least to save my faithful 100-h.p. Mercedes motor from destruction, I sawed and hacked it away from the body. Proof enough of the thoroughness of German handiwork, for it took me fully four hours to detach it.

In order to conform to Neutrality Laws, I handed over the motor to the Mandarin for safe keeping.

Then came the saddest part. As the rest of my machine, even minus planes, could pass through none of the streets or gates of the town, I had to surrender it to the flames. I poured petrol over it, set it alight, and saw it turn to ashes before my eyes.

And as I stood by, watching the holocaust of my poor, brave Taube, I felt as if I were losing a dear and faithful friend.

Chapter Nine

Mr. Macgarvin's Ptomaine Poisoning

In the evening the Mandarin held his reception.

When I stepped out of my door the whole courtyard was ablaze with torches and countless large Chinese lanterns. The guard presented arms, the drums beat and the musicians gave us some tunes – hardly pleasing except to Chinese ears. The Mandarin had even sent me his own palanquin.

I shall never forget that evening. I sat in a litter upholstered in blue silk, with curtained windows, which was carried by eight sturdy fellows. In front, on the sides and behind the palanquin, marched soldiers with fixed bayonets and dozens of runners with paper lanterns. The palanquin swayed gently to the tread of the bearers. Every ten minutes the man at the head gave a loud signal by rapping with his stick on the ground; the litter halted, the bearers moved the carrying poles to the other shoulder, and on we went like the wind.

After forty minutes we reached the Mandarin's palace. Ear-splitting music, shouted orders and the light of many lanterns and torches greeted us. The centre doors of the gigantic portals flew open before me, and in front of the last one the Mandarin himself came forward to receive me.

Several high dignitaries and generals had already assembled, and after ceremonial greetings the ordinary green, thinnish tea was handed round as a sign of welcome. I took advantage of this to present to the Mandarin my Mauser pistol, plus ammunition, as a token of my gratitude. He was visibly pleased, and we sat down to our meal in high good humour. A huge, round table, covered with some fifty dishes, in which swam the daintiest Chinese delicacies, awaited our pleasure. As a specially honoured guest I was handed a knife and fork, and the feast began. I added up the courses, but lost count at the thirty-sixth! But what about the menu? From the delicate swallows' nests to the finest sharks' fins; from sugar-cane salad to the most perfect chicken stews – nothing had been forgotten. I had to sample everything, and the Mandarin was tireless in his attentions, and even sometimes lifted a particular titbit from his own plate to place it with his own fingers on mine! We drank bottled beer from Germany! And German Schnaps.

Mr. Morgan's was the hardest task, for he had to interpret the conversation, which was not devoid of comic aspects.

The battles round Kiao-Chow, the losses of the Japanese and the English and the flying interested the Chinese most of all. Their questions never ran dry.

I took hearty and grateful leave of my Mandarin, and the next day I did the same of my amiable hosts.

When I landed with my aeroplane I had only a tooth-brush, a piece of soap and my flying-kit, *i.e.* my leather jacket, a scarf and leggings. I had also taken a civilian suit with me. I now donned the latter. The five-year-old daughter of our missionary presented me with her old, shabby little felt hat to replace my sports cap, which a Chinese had stolen whilst I was dismantling my machine. And in the evening I was again conducted with ceremony to the junk, which was placed at my disposal.

My suite, and at the same time guard of honour, during the coming journey consisted of the Chinese General Lin, well known as a fighter of pirates, of two officers and forty five men, apart from the crew of the boat. I was terribly worn out after all I had been through, and went to my small wooden room where, to my joy and surprise, instead of the plank bed, I found a beautiful sleeping bag with mattress and blankets, which the attentive wife of the missionary had sent on board for me. Without these I should have come off badly in my thin sports clothes. It was bitterly cold, the wind whistled through the gaps and crannies, and I could see the starry sky through the awning. And whilst my thoughts lingered with my brave comrades in Kiao-Chow, and I gratefully recalled the many battles and dangers I had come through in order to fulfil my task to the end, sleep overtook me and enfolded me in its arms.

The journey proceeded by slow stages.

The junks were dragged upstream by two coolies, by means of a rope which was fastened to our masthead. It took us a day and a half to cover the first stage to Bampu, which I had flown in twenty minutes with my aeroplane. Later on we went faster, especially with a favourable wind filling our sails. But it was only five days later that we arrived at Nanking.

Our progress interested me immensely, for we traversed a criss-cross of rivers to the famous Emperor's Channel, and through this we reached Nanking by way of the Yang-tse-kiang. The country was famous for its pirates, and we passed towns where no European had set foot. During the day, whilst the junk was being towed along, I walked on the bank with the General and some of our guards, and watched with great interest the active and crowded life of these cities, as yet untouched by Western civilization. Chinese men, women and children came running out of their houses, stared in astonishment at the sight of a fair man with blue eyes, who wore no hat. And they sometimes touched my garments to convince themselves that I was really human.

My walks and my life on the junk took a quiet and rather silent course. My courteous General, though he wore European attire, had the typically Chinese bands wound round his ankles, and he sported a fine, long "tail" which was coquettishly tucked under the belt of his jacket. The good man knew not a word of any language but Chinese, and I knew none of that. During our meals, which were of the richest description, but reeked terribly of onions and garlic, we sat opposite each other, and grinned amicably at one another – and that was our whole conversation.

At last, on the 11th of November, we arrived at Yang-dchou-fou, and one can imagine with what avidity I threw myself on the first newspaper.

Pull of excitement in the expectation of hearing at last about the fate of Kiao-Chow, I devoured the pages of the *Shanghai Times*. There on the second page – the name Kiao-Chow. But what was that? Could such treachery exist in the world? For with disgust and loathing of the low English-lying brood, this is what I read:

"The Cowardly Capitulation

of

Kiao-Chow.

The Fortress taken without a Blow.

The Garrison Drunk and Looting."

And after that so much mud, such low-down lying, that I threw the paper aside in disgust. And this was what the English, who had behaved with so little valour before Kiao-Chow, dared assert about our brave defenders!

Ah, but I did not know the English papers then! Later in Shanghai, and also in America, I had to get used to much worse from the American Press, to say nothing of the English. But now, at least, I was certain as to the fate of Kiao-Chow, which was inevitable from the first. I saw also how opportunely I had left the fortress, on the very eve, so to speak, of her forced surrender. We arrived safely at Nanking on the 11th of November 1914.

I was warmly welcomed at the station by Kapitänleutnant Brunner, commander of the torpedo boat S90, and his officers.

We drove in a carriage to the buildings which had been allotted to the officers and crew of the S90 and where to my astonishment, a room was already prepared for me. When I amazedly inquired the reason for this, my comrades told me that I was to be interned, and that they all rejoiced to have a fourth at Skat. I protested loudly that I did not play cards; also, I held my own views on the question of internment, but these I kept to myself.

So I repaired with my General Lin to the palace of the Governor of Nanking. Unfortunately, or rather luckily, we could not see the Governor, and an old Chinese doctor received us very kindly in his stead, and expressed the hope that I should be very happy in Nanking.

I thanked him profusely, though I had no such intention!

I now took leave of my General Lin, who seemed obviously relieved at having concluded his mission; but, when I stepped into my carriage, a fully armed Chinese soldier followed me.

When, astounded, I asked for an explanation, he told me in fairly intelligible German that he was my "Guard of Honour", and had been attached to me for my *protection* and would henceforward accompany me in all my comings and goings.

That was *too* bad! Had I not been formally assured in Hai-Dchou that my removal to Nanking was a pure formality, and that I should be absolutely free?

So they wanted to intern me?

In that case I had to act promptly, before I gave the Chinese the chance to announce this fact to me and rob me of my freedom. The "Guard of Honour" was a nuisance, but I hoped to find means of getting rid of him.

The same evening we were all bidden to the house of a German friend. I had settled on my plan. After a few pleasant hours, during which I had to recount time and again the last days of Kiao-Chow, the other officers took their departure at ten o'clock, followed by their faithful sentries. I stayed on, but after half an hour decided that it was imperative for me to depart, if I still wanted to make my escape.

But when my host stepped out from the house whom did he see? My yellow guardian! We were in a fix; but with prompt decision I sent our "boy" to ask him what he meant by waiting, as all the gentlemen had been gone for a good while, and he would be punished for his carelessness if he did not catch them up.

And whilst the poor devil ran off in their wake, a closed carriage was taking me to the station at breakneck speed. I was just in time to secure the last berth in the newly run express train. The sleeping compartment was already locked, and a tall Englishman opened the door unwillingly and with a furious face, in answer to my spirited knocking. I simply ignored him, jumped into the upper berth, and, turning off the light, pretended to undress. In reality I crept under my pillows and blankets, resolved not to wake up under any provocation. But during the next eight hours I never slept. As often as the train stopped, I felt cold shivers running down my back, saying to myself: "Ha, they will fetch me now!" And, when loud voices sounded outside, I felt convinced that my last train trip during this war was over.

But nothing happened. The. Chinese did not yet seem to have thought of telegraphing in connection with arrests, so, according to schedule, at seven in the morning we arrived in Shanghai. After successfully passing the ticket-collector, I promptly bowled along in a rickshaw through the Chinese quarter – where the Chinese authorities still had a hold on me – and at last reached the European side, where I felt safe and free from interference.

I went straight to a German acquaintance, who received me with open arms, and whose guest I remained during the next three weeks.

For it was fully that before I was able to continue my journey; and in the meantime how many adventures, perils, and games of hide-and-seek!

For what was more natural than that Oberleutnant P. should not be known at all at my quarters, and that Herr Meyer, who had stayed there for a few days, should already have left?

That Mr. Scott had come on a visit to his kind friends, of course, was no one's business. But prudence was essential, especially as I knew a great number of people in Shanghai, many of whom were English, met previously in Kiao-Chow before the war.

I assumed four or five different names, and stayed with different friends in succession.

But the greatest difficulty still lay in finding ways and means to get to America. Once I nearly got away on an *English* ship, thanks to the introduction which a German friend procured for me. An English shipowner introduced me as a Swiss, who did not know *one* word of English. I listened to the whole conversation, but was able to suppress my jubilation when I heard that I was to sail on the steamer *Goliath*, bound direct for San Francisco. It was, alas, of short duration, for the ship had weighed anchor two hours earlier on account of the tide – and we came too late!

I could have tried another steamer, but they all went by way of Japan, and I feared to risk that.

Fortune, however, smiled upon me. One day I accidentally met a friend with whom I had spent many a gay night in the haunts of the Far East; he was at once ready to help me. And after only a few days I held the necessary papers, and had received all the needful instructions. From a Mr. Scott, Meyer or Brown, I turned suddenly into a distinguished Englishman, rolling in money, who bore the beautiful and dignified name of MacGarvin. This gentleman was representative of the Singer Sewing Machines Company, and on his way from Shanghai to his factories in California.

What was more natural for Mr. MacGarvin than to travel on one of the first outgoing American Mail Steamers!

There were only two luxurious staterooms aboard this boat. The one was allotted to an American multi-millionaire, the other to Oberleutnant Plüschow – no, I mean, Mr. MacGarvin. One difficulty still remained: to escape unobserved from Shanghai.

But there my friends again came to the rescue. Three days before the ship sailed I took official leave, and spread the report that I no longer felt safe in Shanghai, and was going to Peking, in order to work there at the German Legation. At eleven that night I left in a carriage for the station. How could I be expected to know that the coachman turned off a few minutes before, and drove sharply out of the town in a southern direction? What did I know about Shanghai?

After we had rolled along the Wusung River for nearly two hours, we stopped. Two men armed with revolvers came up, a brief countersign was exchanged; with deep respect and gratitude I kissed a woman's slim, white hands which were extended to me from the interior of the carriage, and it wheeled round and disappeared. My two friends took me in their midst, I also drew my revolver, and we stepped silently into the waiting junk.

The night was black as pitch, the wind howled, and the dirty, dark water gurgled dismally as it flew by, driven by the tide.

The four Chinks bent to their sculls with the utmost exertion, and after an hour we reached our destination, which lay many miles down-stream on the opposite shore!

Soundlessly we landed, soundlessly the junk disappeared; and in the same fashion we made our way towards a dark building which stood in the midst of a small garden near some huge factories.

My eyes were blinded by the glare of many electric lamps, once the door had been carefully locked after us.

I soon noticed that we were in comfortable bachelor's quarters. The table was spread, and we courageously attacked the many delicious dishes. Over this meal we decided on our tactics.

The apartment belonged to the two young men who worked during the day at the factory. The servants were pure Chinese, which was all to the good.

My visit had to be kept secret in any case, especially as a disagreeable individual, who belonged to the "Entente", also lived on the premises.

It was our intention to take advantage of the fear which the Chinese profess for evil spirits, and especially of their superstition in regard to mad people. Therefore, my problem was to act the part of a madman for three days.

I was given a tiny room, where I was locked in. The "boy" received detailed and sharp instructions from his master, and so I felt secure that I should not be betrayed.

Dash it all! I never thought it would be so difficult to feign madness. For three days I remained shut up in this room, raved and stamped about, sometimes dropping into a chair and staring stupidly in front of me.

As soon as the "boy", who was on guard outside, noticed these symptoms, he carefully opened the door and pushed through his tray with food like greased lightning, then withdrew his arm, and I could feel with what relief he turned the key on me on the outside. When I sometimes burst out laughing, because I felt in such high spirits, the poor chap must have thought I had a fresh attack.

At last, on the evening of the third day, we left the house silently and cautiously.

A large steamer lay near the landing place, we took brief but warm leave of each other, and off we went in the direction of the Wusung Roadstead.

The weather was bad, the sea rough and the gangway was not even let down. After calling and yelling loudly, at last somebody appeared and helped Mr, MacGarvin to board the ship with his solitary trunk.

Nobody even looked at me. The deck was in half-darkness, and at last I went up to several of the officers and inquired as to the whereabouts of my cabin. Something unintelligible was growled at me, but when the gentlemen looked more closely at my ticket a sudden change took place. Bowings and scrapings and fluent excuses. A blast from the whistle of an officer, and several stewards appeared as by magic, headed by the white head steward. The deck lamps gleamed. The stewards fought over the possession of my trunk, and the head steward conducted me with *empressement* to my state room. He simply exuded politeness.

"Oh, Mr. MacGarvin, why do you come today? The steamer only leaves the day after to-morrow, and it was known all over Shanghai at midday!"

I looked furious, and expressed my indignation that the owner of a state cabin should not have been warned in time.

He was followed by my fat Chinese cabin steward, who was repose and distinction personified. But he put me into a fix.

One of his "boys" was ordered to bring my trunk, whereupon he asked me, in doubting tones, whether this represented all my luggage.

"Yes," I said.

He supposed my other trunks were in the hold.

"Of course. My heavy luggage was brought on board yesterday, and I hope that my valuable belongings were carefully handled."

Oh, if the good Chink had guessed how proud I was of that *one* trunk, even though it was suspiciously light!

At last, on the 5th of December 1914, the steamer *Mongolia* weighed anchor.

In spite of the lovely weather and good food, on the very next day Mr. MacGarvin was suddenly taken ill. He himself did know what it was. Probably severe ptomaine poisoning, and the ship's doctor was quickly sent for. He was a brilliant man, a thorough sportsman and ready for any joke. His concerned face took on an astonished expression when, instead of a patient at death's door, he beheld my florid and sunburnt countenance.

I had confidence in him, and in a few words I explained my situation. I have seldom seen anyone's eyes gleam with such pleasure as his did after I had confessed my sins to him. His uproarious laugh and warm handshake convinced me that I had chanced on the right man. The steward knocked at the door.

The ship's surgeon assumed an anxious mien, whilst I groaned. The steward flitted in, and the American said to him in hushed, impressive tones: "Look here, Boy! This Master plenty ill, don't disturb him, can't get up before ten days; give him plenty good food, chosen by cook; always bring to him in bed. If Master want anything, you call me!"

During this speech I already held one end of the blanket in my mouth, and if it had lasted longer I would have swallowed the whole. Once more I took the centre of the stage.

Three days on the sea, and then came the first of the three Japanese harbours which I dreaded. The steamer ran peacefully into Nagasaki, and immediately a flood of custom-officers, policemen and detectives inundated the boat. The bell rang through the ship, and summoned passengers and crew for examination. And now the whole procedure started. The passengers were assembled in the saloon. Each was called by name; man, woman and child questioned by a commission consisting of police officers and detectives; their papers closely examined; and they themselves overhauled by the Japanese doctor with regard to infectious diseases. Above all, they wanted to know which of them came from Kiao-Chow. The thirty-fifth name called was that of MacGarvin. Every one looked round, for, of course, no one had even seen him. Whereupon the ship's surgeon approached, looked very serious, and whispered some dreadful news into the ear of his Japanese colleague.

Some fifteen minutes later I heard a hum of many voices before my cabin. The door was carefully opened. In walked the American ship's surgeon, and in his wake crept two Japanese police officers and the Japanese doctor. The poor victim of ptomaine poisoning lay in a huddled heap, moaning softly, and with nothing to be seen of him but a crop of hair.

The American came close to the bed and lightly touched my shoulder, which apparently called forth horrible pain. He immediately stepped back and whispered: "Oh, very ill, very ill!" The Japs, who had from the first contemplated the beautifully furnished cabin with shy admiration, seemed happy to get out of these unwonted surroundings. They kow-towed profoundly, hissed something through their teeth, which was meant to express particular deference, a softly murmured "Oh, I beg your pardon!" and the entire Yellow Peril disappeared from my sight.

I believe that during this whole scene, and just before, I did feel a slight attack of the shivers – but it did not last.

In the afternoon I risked getting up for a moment as I wanted to catch a glimpse of Nagasaki, which I already knew.

But the sight that met my eyes sent me scuttling back to my bunk. The harbour was filled with countless steamers, richly festooned with flags. Extraordinary animation reigned aboard the ships; troops, horses and guns were being put ashore continuously.

The soldiers were in gala attire, and the houses of the town nearly disappeared under the load of garlands and flags; a huge crowd flowed through the streets to the parade-ground, where a review was to be held. So these were the conquerors of Kiao-Chow!

The whole of Japan fêted today the defeat and humiliation of the German Empire. I read that night in the Japanese papers, which appeared in English, that Japan had achieved that which the English, French and Russians had tried in vain – to defeat Germany; and that from now onwards their army was the best and the strongest in the whole world. But enough of this, the Americans and the English have not shown greater restraint on other occasions.

Twice more the steamer ran into harbour during the next days. Both at Kobe and Yokohama my cabin witnessed the same procedure as at Nagasaki – Mr. MacGarvin remained ill and unmolested.

We stayed five days in all in Japan. At last, after I had kept to my bunk for a whole week, we left those dangerous shores. And when they disappeared on the horizon a young man on the steamer is said to have danced with joy and frantically waved a small hat, which had belonged to a little girl in far away China, shouting laughingly: "Good-bye, Japs! Good-bye, Japs!"

The days passed pleasantly enough amidst the recreations which are usual on board an ocean-going steamer. I met several Germans, whom the war had thrust forth from their adopted country; also a brother officer who had been lately busy at Shanghai, and a war comrade: the American war correspondent, Mr. Brace, who was the only foreigner to take part in the whole siege of Kiao-Chow.

Neptune took care to provide us with a change. Shortly before Honolulu, we were caught in a typhoon, which lasted nearly two days and threatened our ship with dire peril.

When we arrived in Honolulu the sun was shining brightly, and I had to look twice before I dared trust my eyes. For did I not see the German war flag!

And as we dropped anchor there lay alongside, like a tiny cockleshell, the small cruiser *Geier* which, coming from the South Seas, had run the blockade and had just been interned. What a curious meeting! I met dear comrades again from whom I had heard nothing for a long time, in the midst of war, far from our country, after momentous happenings. We talked and talked without end.

At the beginning of the war the *Geier* lay far away to the south amongst the coral reefs. She only heard of the Russian mobilization, then her wireless went to pieces, and she swam about without news in the Pacific. Only fourteen days later, the *Geier* heard something of the war with England and later with Japan. This meant caution. Surrounded and hunted by a score of enemies, the small cruiser achieved a voyage of many thousands of sea miles to Honolulu, either taken in tow by a small steamer or sailing on her own. And when the huge Japanese cruiser, which lay on the watch for her at the mouth of the harbour, one fine morning beheld the cockleshell safe in port, with the German flag flying at the masthead, the yellow monkey had to slink off homewards with its tail between its legs.

After our departure from Honolulu I had a bone to pick with my war correspondent. Beaming with joy, he brought me the *Honolulu Times* and proudly showed me the first page, on which my name, my profession and my nationality were recorded in immense letters, followed by several columns of close print, which recounted all my misdeeds during and after the siege of Kiao-Chow.

Truly American this – to be judged according to what the papers said.

But the whole business was extremely painful to me, for I had every reason to fear that the American authorities would arrest me on my arrival at San Francisco on the strength of this report. However, all the Americans on board reassured me and expressed their opinion that I would be allowed to go my own way without hindrance. For what I had done was "good sport". On the contrary, people in America would be delighted at my adventures, and if I only behaved sensibly, and gave up my foolish German militarist ideas, I could make a lot of money there. The thing for me to do was to apply to the right kind of newspaper. It would take the matter in hand, arrange for the needful publicity, and then I could travel from town to town – possibly preceded by a band – and collect "plenty dollars". Those Americans were truly gifted with fine feelings! One of these gentlemen, a jolly old man, who had a charming daughter with him, came to me one day and took me seriously in hand.

"Now look here, Mr. MacGarvin, I like you; I take an interest in your career. What are you going to do now? You have probably no money. You are unknown in America, and it is difficult to find a job there!"

"Well, I want to return to Germany and fight for my country, as I am an officer."

He smiled with pity.

"You will never be able to get out of America. And with all respect for your confidence in your country and your enthusiasm – believe me, I have good connections over there – in a few months Germany will be annihilated, and then you will neither get work nor be allowed to live there. England will allow no German officer to remain in Germany when the war is over. They will all be deported. The German Empire will be divided, and the Kaiser deposed by his own people. Do be sensible; try to make a new home for yourself and stay in America. I am quite ready to help you."

But that was too much. My patience was exhausted, and I gave the gentleman an answer which taught him many new things about German officers and the real state of affairs in Germany. In the end he was quite converted to my ideas, and showed himself still more amiable towards me. Subsequently I was often his guest in San Francisco and New York.

On the 30th of December we cast anchor in San Francisco.

A typically American reception.

Dozens of newspaper reporters and photographers swarmed over the deck, filled the saloons, and even invaded the cabins. The fellows had already got on my scent. They surrounded one on all sides; cameras clicked everywhere – it was simply revolting. At last I took refuge in the only .expedient that is of any use. I became rude and shouted: "I have nothing to say, and if you molest me any further I shall fetch the police." My war correspondent from Kiao-Chow had taught me beforehand to treat his colleagues in this manner.

Only a tiny yellow Japanese crept up to me like a cat, made a deep obeisance, hissed through his teeth and said, with a false smile, that he came from the Japanese Consulate (of all places!) to greet me and to wish me happiness on my leaving Kiao-Chow with such luck. He assured me I had nothing to fear, as I was on American soil; but that he would be only too charmed to send a short account to his paper in Tokio, to delight his Japanese brethren.

I ordered my Chinese steward to throw the yellow Jap out.

San Francisco!

Chapter Ten

Caught!

San Francisco! Oh, huge, marvellous city!

What I enjoyed most was my freedom from arrest. Officialdom did not take the slightest notice of my presence, and I remained there for several days, in spite of the frantic anxiety of the German Consulate, which expected me to be led into captivity at any moment. I have rarely in my life enjoyed a madder, more delirious New Year's Eve than in San Francisco! Nothing that I had heard about it approached reality. It was a pleasure to look at the people – thoroughbred, every one of them. The men tall and strong, the women captivatingly beautiful in their blonde fairness. My friends invited me to one of their biggest and most beautiful night clubs. Exorbitant prices and the smartest society of San Francisco. During that night everything seemed permissible.

The music and the dancing carried one away with their beauty and wildness. It was the night of San Francisco.

On the 2nd of January 1915 I took my departure, and by chance I met in the same railway carriage one of my comrades, and also several Germans with whom I had previously travelled by boat. We had a most enjoyable journey, the more so as the papers brought good news from Germany. As several of the elderly ladies and gentlemen were bound for home, we two officers also firmly believed that we were not far from attaining our object.

We stopped at the Great Canyon of Arizona to admire the mighty wonders of Nature, which enfolded themselves in their glorious beauty. On the following days our train sped through the prairie, recalling to our minds boyish recollections of Fenimore Cooper and the Mohicans. At Chicago we separated, and I travelled thence to Virginia on a visit to dear friends of mine, and in the hope of finding out how I best could reach Europe.

After two or three days I sped to New York to try my luck there.

I had to hang about in New York for fully three weeks, and during these I had many opportunities of studying its people and their customs. Three weeks, in which time after time I nearly burst with fury. It was the climax of all I had endured until then. Hardly a picture, hardly a newspaper, hardly an advertisement that did not incite hatred against Germany, that did not pour abuse on the brave German soldiers. "Tipperary" seemed to have become the National Anthem of New York.

Was there no one who could open the eyes of these people? Did they really not *wish* to see and hear the truth? But the majority knew Germany only from hearsay – they hardly even knew where Germany was; and in spite of this they were ready with their judgment. Here one could gauge the monstrous power of the lying English Press, and the crass stupidity with which the Americans swallowed the bait. I did what I could. I talked, and explained, and tried to convince, but met everywhere the same answer: "Of course, *you* would not commit these atrocities; but your countrymen, Huns and Barbarians, do nothing else. Here it is, black on white in the *Times* – a paper of that importance does not tell lies." My greatest consolation during that time was the touching manner in which I was treated and received by my friends and their acquaintances, and I remain truly grateful to them. One night I was particularly enraged. I had been to the Metropolitan Opera House, where I had listened to one act from *Hänsel und Gretel* – German music, German words and German songs! My heart was bursting with frantic, aching longing for my beloved country; my soul drank in long draughts of German melody. Still bemused and carried away by my feelings, I stepped into the street and found myself at once recalled to reality.

The big space in front of the theatre held a huge crowd, as it did every night, and a cinema projector threw the newest war bulletins in garish letters across a blank wall. As was to be expected, Russia had again achieved one of her famous victories. The English had annihilated the army of the Crown Prince! The crowd was yelling with delight. Battle pictures followed. First some English and French warships, then suddenly, the German cruiser *Goeben*. The people raved, whistled, hissed, shouted – the din was endless. So much for the *neutral* Americans, so anxious to uphold the rights of men and the ends of Justice!

Until now all my efforts to reach Europe had been fruitless. I had imagined that my task would be easier. Once I nearly succeeded in sailing on a Norwegian boat as an ordinary sailor; but was dissuaded, as there were several Englishmen in her crew. At last I got what I wanted. By chance I made the acquaintance of a man who had led a rather stormy existence. He had been all over the world, and had lived for a long time in New York. I was never really quite able to ascertain his real occupation. However, he was very successful at one particular job – which consisted in polishing up old passports. We quickly concluded our bargain. In a few hours I had my papers with my photograph neatly pasted in, and all the proper police notifications entered according to existing regulations. And in this wise the Swiss traveller, locksmith, Ernst Suse, went on board the neutral Italian steamboat *Duca degli Abruzzi* on the 30th of January 1915, and disappeared into the steerage.

Two hours later we passed the statue of Liberty. Five sea miles out of New York two English cruisers were watching the mouth of the harbour. A shining example of the Freedom of the Seas! The journey was abominable. Though I had been trained in a rough school as a naval officer aboard a T.B.D. I had never dreamed of anything like it. The ship was heavily overweighted, and pitched and tossed to such a degree that I was convinced that she would capsize under the impact of the heavy seas. And the bugs! But I shall go into that later. On the morning of the third day of our journey I stood on deck and gazed longingly at the first class railings over which two charming little faces were looking down at me. A gentleman approached them, and with difficulty I suppressed the name which sprang to my lips. For I knew him; it was—

Doubt was impossible. It was my brother officer T., who had come with me from Shanghai. He saw me at the same moment, but only recognized me after he had exchanged some very loud remarks with the ladies about the filthy fellow down below (meaning myself). Suddenly he stopped, stared hard at me, smiled knowingly, after which he suddenly turned away and disappeared.

In the evening, when darkness had completely fallen, I had an opportunity of a short talk with him. He was travelling as a distinguished Dutchman (of course he did not speak a single word of Dutch), and his destination, like mine, was Naples, and from thence homewards. Though we had both met daily in New York, each intent on getting home, we had been obliged by our respective helpers to keep what we did a dead secret from each other. And we now learned that we had both been to the same man!

Some days after leaving New York I suddenly went down with a high temperature, and had to take to my bed. I did not know what was the matter with me, but presumed malaria, and so did the Italian doctor, who gave me a ridiculously large dose of quinine. I did not have to wait long for the result, as I promptly grew worse, and my temperature rose to 103°. These days were indescribable. Our cabin, a veritable hole, was shared by four passengers. Above me lay a Frenchman who only stopped gabbling and cursing when he was sea-sick. The lower berth was occupied by a pale and resigned Swiss (his nationality at once awoke my suspicions). This man was so sea-sick that it was my opinion he would never reach Europe alive. In the upper, left hand berth a perfectly rabid Englishman smoked his pipe of Player's Navy Cut unremittingly day and night, in spite of the closed portholes. He was nearly always drunk and unable to cease his abuse and revilings against Germany for one moment. It is easy to imagine how much rest I got! To cap it all, my berth lay close to the engines, and the bugs were the worst item of the programme. And these dreadful pests did not come singly, but in battalions. Oh, what were the noises, the horrible smells and the sea-sickness compared to this plague! In spite of my exhausting weakness I tried to destroy or to drive away the loathsome insects. But I was soon forced to give up in despair.

After that I relapsed into complete indifference. I told myself that the voyage would be over in a few days, and as soon as we had reached beautiful Italy, and I had given myself a short rest, I should be back in my beloved Fatherland. I fought off my illness with the utmost energy, and the thought of Germany aided my convalescence, so that when the ship reached Gibraltar on the 8th of February I was able to be up and about.

Gibraltar!

How many times already had I sailed past this Rock, how often had I, returning from foreign parts, tendered joyous welcome to the grey stones, the sign post, in these straits to the faithful homeland! What was in store for me this time? In spite of the fact that the time-table made no provision for calling at Gibraltar, the ship entered the port for examination, without even awaiting a request to do so, and dropped anchor. To this extent had the Italians already become the slaves of the English! As soon as the ship lay to, two pinnaces descended upon us, from which emerged an English naval officer and sundry policemen and sailors armed to the teeth. A bell was sounded all over the ship, with the order that all foreign passengers, who were neither English nor Italian, should assemble on the pilot bridge. The Italian stewards went below, inspected the ship's hold and all the cabins, and drove us like a herd of sheep to the upper deck, where we were closely surrounded by them and the English sailors. I cannot pretend that I felt particularly happy! In spite of this I experienced a certain amount of confidence, as I soon found out that I was the only one equipped with a genuine passport and photograph. On the other hand, I established the fact that we were five Swiss, three of whom had already excited my suspicion on account of their shy and retiring disposition. There was only one whom I had not noticed at all, and he looked so dirty and repulsive that I took the precaution of moving away when he placed himself beside me. After an hour, during which the first class passengers were examined – casually, and with great politeness – our turn came. We stood there like six miserable sinners. The first one was an Italian-Swiss workman, who had lost his right arm. His wife, a typical Italian, prostrated herself wailingly at the Englishman's feet. She was accompanied from the steerage by her whole tribe, and they *all* wailed. The Englishman looked contemptuously at those people, and after a short examination the man was dismissed and free to go. We had now to advance. The tallest amongst us Swiss stood on the right wing. The English officer went up to him and said: "You are a German officer." Violent and indignant protestations naturally followed; but the English officer, whom they left quite cool, ordered him aside and turned to us – we seemed more like the genuine article in his sight. We pointed to our passports, and each one of us dished up a wondrous yarn. After a short pause he said: "All right; these four can go, but I will keep that one."

My heart was throbbing with joy, but, alas, then appeared the Judas. A young fellow, in perfectly fitting civilian clothes, went up to the officer and spoke to him in raised tones. "It is quite out of the question that these people should be allowed to leave without having all their belongings thoroughly searched. I am convinced they are Germans." We exclaimed loudly at this, but to no end, though the English officer obeyed this blackguard with evident reluctance and contempt. However, the examination took place. Everything was turned upside down. The rascal ferreted about everywhere, but seemed unable to find any incriminating marks on any of our belongings. Suddenly he whipped round; tore open my coat, turned out my breast-pockets and said triumphantly to the officer who stood at his side, "You see, there is neither a name nor a monogram. It is a sure sign that he is a German, and that he has destroyed all initials." Oh, if I could but have brained the reptile!

As we were soon to learn, this civilian was the representative of the firm of Thomas Cook Brothers [sic] in Gibraltar, and acted on the ships in the dual capacity of d— spy and interpreter. His German was so pure that he must have enjoyed our hospitality in Germany for many years. How many wretched creatures probably owe their undoing to this busybody!

Once more we five were driven on deck like cattle. At this moment Judas number two appeared, who had been fetched by the Cook's agent. This was a first class Swiss passenger, and at the instigation of the arch sneak he was to try us in Swiss dialect. Of course we all failed miserably. Our protests were useless. Not even when I told them the wildest tales about knowing no German, as I had left Switzerland with my parents when a child of three, and had settled with them in Italy, and that after that I had drifted to America. I talked nineteen to the dozen in good Italian and American, and I nearly succeeded; but the snake hissed again – and my hopes were dashed to the ground.

The English officer refused us any further hearing; but only remarked that more Swiss had passed through Gibraltar than there were in the whole world. Bursting with a frenzy that bordered on madness, I was led away. I quickly gathered my few traps and was able unobserved to slip a scrap of paper into a German lady's hand, which she later faithfully delivered to my relatives. A sailor rudely propelled me down the gangway into the pinnace, where the other poor wretches already sat, completely crushed. On the arrival of the English officer with his minion we started.

The Swiss traitor stood at the breast-rail of the ship and grinned gloatingly at us. Thereupon I was unable to contain myself any longer, but jumped up and shook my fist at him, yelling out an invective. Hysterical, treacherous laughter sounded back.

But a pair of German eyes sent me a sad farewell from starboard.

Goodbye, oh, happy comrade! Greet for me the Fatherland you will see again in a few days.

Chapter Eleven

Behind Walls and Barbed Wire

The English officer reassured me. "Be assured," he said, "that you will be able to interview your Swiss Consul at Gibraltar today. You will be free the moment he confirms that your passport is in order."

I was only too soon to learn how matters stood in regard to this. The steam launch churned its way through the water, and soon we disembarked in the inner part of the war harbour.

Ten soldiers with fixed bayonets stood ready at the landing stage. A few curt orders and, with our few belongings on our backs, we had to fall in in two files. The ten soldiers took us into their midst, and at the word "Quick march" the sad procession set out on its way. Everything around me seemed part of a dream. I was so horribly downcast that I was hardly able to think. A prisoner! Was it true? Was it possible?

It was horrible, incomprehensible! We were being led along like malefactors, and the population seemed to regard us as such. The soldiers told us to hurry up. I was so weak that I could hardly move, as the fever still held me in its grip and I had taken nothing except quinine for the last three days. The sun beat down on our backs, and I had never felt more desolate or more hopeless.

We climbed higher and higher, through narrow, hot streets. Soon the houses gave place to bare rocks on either side. After an hour we had reached the highest summit of Gibraltar. Orders rang out, barbed-wire fences and iron doors opened and clanged to, chains and bolts rattled.

A prisoner!

We were first brought to the police station, and there subjected to an examination. I protested with energy and demanded to be taken at once to my Consul, as I had definitely been promised this by the English officer. But they laughed regretfully. We were not the first, alas, that had been brought before them and had made this same request! How many had probably stood in the same place and been obliged to bury their hopes in the same way!

After that examination we had to submit to being searched.

"Have any of the prisoners got money?"

Of course no one answered. We were ordered to undress, and every garment was closely searched for money, cameras and especially letters and papers. I came third, and was allowed to keep my shirt on.

"Have you got any money?"

"No."

The sergeant major passed his hands all over my body. Suddenly something chinked in the left-hand pocket of my shirt.

"What is this?"

"I don't know."

He now plunged his paw right in, and what did he extract? A beautiful twenty-dollar piece of the best American gold, and also a small mother-of-pearl button, which had betrayed me by knocking against the coin. This comes of being too tidy! Had I thrown it away two days before, instead of hoarding it carefully, this would not have happened. The English soldier rejoiced, for such finds did not occur every day. But now he examined me more thoroughly. And to my distress he extracted from my other breast pocket, as well as from each of the two trouser pockets, a lovely golden piece and my small Browning revolver, which had been my faithful companion all these months.

When I had been completely despoiled I was allowed to dress again and to rejoin my comrades in misfortune in the prison yard. After that we took possession of our quarters. About fifty German civilian prisoners greeted us uproariously. They had been in captivity ever since the beginning of the war, and seemed to have recovered their sense of humour. Our new friends invited us at once to share their meal. We threw ourselves like savages on the bread pudding which they had prepared for themselves.

Then we started on our work.

In the first place, we were made to carry coal and water. We were detailed according to height, and accidentally I fell in with the dirty Swiss whom I had already regarded with such repulsion on the ship.

In the meanwhile we went on dragging sacks of coal, and we were careful not to fill the bins to their full capacity. Were we not too weak to do so properly? After we had carried on this job for some time we were allotted our soldiers' mattresses, consisting of three parts, and as hard as stone; also two blankets. We were allowed to rest that evening. But the first thing was to get a wash. I well recall the scene.

My filthy colleague placed his basin near mine, and stripped with the utmost placidity. Hang it all! I had not expected so much cleanliness, and inspected him critically. A perfectly shaped body and clean – spotlessly clean! But head, neck and hands! I shuddered. And then I stopped in the midst of my ablutions. My eyes opened wide in astonishment. The water of my colleague was coal-black; but he was completely metamorphosed. His black, oily hair had turned into shining blonde, his face looked fresh and white, and showed delicate features, the hands were slim and elegant. And was it possible? Across the cheek and the temple ran the honourable scars of students' duels – real German scars! Such an explosion of joy! Such a cross fire of questions and answers! My comrade had been a *real* German student, was now at the head of a good motor car business in America, and had left it all to serve his country as an officer in the Reserve. We chummed up quickly, and remained faithful, inseparable friends through all the weeks of our captivity, until fate separated us once more.

The last post sounded at ten – lights out followed.

I had placed my mattress near a French window, so that I could easily look through it whilst lying on the floor. The day had brought many changes, and only now was I able to reflect on them.

The barracks in which we were quartered lay at the very top of Gibraltar, on the south, where the rocks drop straight into the sea.

Through the window I saw, deep below me, the wonderfully blue waters of the Straits of Gibraltar; quite far away on the horizon, the coast of Africa, a fine and shining strip of land. Down below was Liberty, ships wended their way to and fro, carrying men, free and unfettered, who could travel where they liked and – who did not appreciate how marvellous and precious it was to be free!

But that way madness lay!

The thoughts and events of the day raced through my brain, and when I remembered that, with luck, I might have been on one of these boats I nearly burst with rage. And it was my birthday too! Well, I had planned it otherwise.

Like a madman I rolled about on my couch. When I thought of how different things might have been, of all I had hoped for, and how I had pictured my future, I gave way to utter despair, and helpless fury brought the tears coursing down my cheeks without my being able to check them.

Oh, longing for home – dreadful longing! But during that night I was not the only sufferer.

Pale faces with wide-open eyes stared at the ceiling, and suppressed sobbing was smothered in the blankets. The next morning, at four o'clock, we were suddenly awakened. The English non commissioned officers went through the rooms and yelled out an order that all German prisoners had to get ready to march off in twenty minutes' time to sail by the next boat to England.

To England! But that was impossible! Were we not Swiss? Had we not to see our Consul on that very day? All our efforts broke against the stolid, imperturbable calm of the English. We quickly collected our property and, exactly half an hour later, the civilian prisoners, numbering fifty six, surrounded by a hundred heavily armed English soldiers, were marched out into the bright morning.

But we wanted to prove to the English that our pride was unbroken. With a clear and ringing sound, intensified by the anger that was burning within us, we poured forth "The Watch on the Rhine", flinging its notes up to the skies.

A huge transport, filled to overflowing with English troops, awaited us below. We had to run the gauntlet through a narrow passage that was formed for us in the great crowd of travellers and those who had come to see them off. But I must admit that nobody molested us, and that no word of disparagement reached our ears. Room for us was made in silence, in silence we were allowed to pass, even here and there we encountered a look of commiseration and regret. On board, in the front part of the cargo deck, a space had been partitioned off and sparsely furnished with benches, tables and hammocks.

There stood two sentries with fixed bayonets; there was another couple near the hatch over our heads. When the latter was closed down from outside, we sat as in a trap. The portholes of our habitation were blinded by iron shutters, so that none of us should be able to look out or flash signals. After a short time a slight tremor ran through the ship, the engines started, and our swimming prison, rising and sinking slightly, drifted out into the open sea.

The journey lasted for days. We sat, closely guarded, shut up in our room. Once a day we were allowed on deck to get a breath of fresh air. A most primitive lavatory had been erected on the fore deck with a few boards, and whoever wanted to use it had to report himself to the sentry. Only one person at a time was allowed to appear on deck for this purpose. The food was good – real sailors' rations – especially the bread, the butter and the abundant supply of excellent jam. We beguiled the time away by reading, story telling; above all, we discussed our future from all points of view, and what lay in store for us in England. The two sentries, who always kept watch below, soon became quite friendly, and we often frightened the poor Tommies into fits by tales of what happened on the Western Front.

Rough weather greeted us in the Bay of Biscay. It was a dreadful state of affairs for the fifty six of us shut up in that restricted space, without light or air, and the majority sea sick. The sentries, and the English soldiers who brought us our food, however, suffered most, and presented a pitiful spectacle. But when we got into the Channel the crew was seized with general nervousness and agitation. Drills with lifebelts were held daily, our recreation hour on deck was suspended, and the English soldiers never stopped questioning us fearfully in regard to our U-boats! And didn't we make it hot for them!

At last, after ten days, we landed at Plymouth. When the chain cable rattlingly uncoiled itself, and we knew that we were safe in port and had escaped U-boats, we watched through the bulkhead the English soldiers falling on their knees and singing hymns of praise and gratitude for their salvation from the German submarines.

Immediately after our arrival a tender came alongside and conveyed us to terra firma—of course under imposing escort.

The English authorities were evidently unprepared for such a *large* consignment of prisoners. They simply lost their heads. No one knew what to do with us, no one what to advise.

At last we were packed into a train. I got a compartment to myself, flanked on either side by a non-commissioned officer, and with another one sitting opposite me, with fixed bayonets. They had been given strict injunctions to watch me carefully, for the following reason: when I saw that it was quite impossible that I should be set free or recognized as a Swiss, I had reported myself to my Commanding Officer in my true colours, the others doing likewise. He assured me that he would transfer me at once to the first class, if I would give him my parole never to try to escape or to fight again in the war. As I naturally rejected this demand with the utmost indignation, I was sent back to the cargo deck, the only result being a stricter surveillance.

In the evening, at dusk, we reached Portsmouth. At the station and elsewhere this huge quantity of prisoners (we were fifty six in all) seemed to bewilder everybody completely.

At last we were marched off to the lock up. There also we found great bewilderment and confusion. The lock up usually affords a temporary domicile to drunken soldiers and sailors who are picked up in the streets, and who have an opportunity of sleeping off their intoxication until the next day, when they are sent back to their platoon after a sound thrashing [*sic*]. An old, obnoxious jailer, and two elderly but jovial and kindly soldiers, were in charge. We were disposed of in three rooms. They were totally empty, and lit by a miserable gas jet. The window panes were mostly broken, it was bitterly cold, and there was, of course, no fire. We had eaten nothing all day, and were looking forward to our supper, but there was no supper. Thereupon we approached our two old soldiers and promptly sealed our pact of friendship. A small tip acted miraculously – the old fogies simply scampered off on our errands. We gave them money, and in half an hour they returned, groaning under a load of bread, butter and cold meat. Two huge pots of tea, mixed with milk and sugar, made their appearance. We got some charcoal ourselves, and soon the three fireplaces were ablaze. The provisions were excellent, and so abundant that even we, famished as we were, could not deal with the lot.

Our spirits reached their zenith when the soldiers slipped us in a few English newspapers. Our mental hunger had been greater than our physical needs, as for weeks we had heard nothing whatsoever about the happenings of the outer world. We did not mind reading exclusively of English, French and Russian victories, as long as we at least knew something of what was going on.

Alcohol was forbidden; but even in England rules seemed made only to be broken. One of our warders belonged to a masonic lodge, members of which were widely distributed over England and America. My colleague, the locksmith, happened to be Master. When the soldier saw the Freemasons' sign in my friend's buttonhole, their pact was sealed. A small canteen flourished in the basement of our prison, and one after another we were led down by the kindly brother, and returned thence fortified with pockets bulging with beer bottles.

The joke was that our sentries, who stood on guard before our door, allowed us to go away quietly, and even begged us to bring them up a few bottles of beer. At 9 p.m. our sentries had become so chummy that we practised rifle exercises together, and at 11 p.m. one sentry dropped his rifle altogether and tumbled backwards, with the coal-box, on which he had been sitting, atop of him.

If I had possessed the experience which was mine after five months' captivity, I should have escaped even then.

In this prison, as well as in all other camps where we foregathered with the English Tommies, their first request, after we had become better acquainted, was for a little note with our address and possibly the address of friends in Germany, and an attestation that the English soldier so-and-so had treated us well. These notes were treasured by them as relics, to be produced at the Front, or in case of capture by the Germans.

We were given tiny camp palliasses, which were so short that our legs projected from the calves downwards, and so narrow that it would have taken an ingenious circus performer to balance his back on it. We also had two blankets each. We slept like logs, though, it is true, the next morning found us all on the floor alongside the mattresses.

On the following morning – it was Sunday – we received the visit of an army officer of high rank. He inquired after our wishes. I pointed out repeatedly that I was an officer, and had the right to be treated as a prisoner of war. He was most charming, and promised me many things when we should arrive at our destination – but kept none of them.

At last, on the Monday, we were allowed to leave our prison. As usual, closely guarded by our escort, we were marched to the harbour, where we boarded a small steamer, and after an hour's journey reached a huge ship which was used as a prisoners' camp. After a long palaver we were obliged to put out to sea again, for the Commandant declared that he had no information about us, and no room either. Though this comedy was re-enacted on the next steamer, the Cunard liner *Andania*, the fluency of our Major's vituperations probably surpassed that of the Camp Commandant's; anyway, we went on board after half an hour's delay. A fat, bumptious, English lieutenant, who filled the post of Camp Commandant and interpreter on this boat, received us.

When my turn came to be inspected I politely presented my request, and forcibly demanded that, according to regulations, I should be taken to an officers' camp. The answer of this gentleman was quite unprecedented, and showed up his vulgarity.

"I shall treat you with special severity, as I have already heard about you. You bolted from Kiao-Chow, and have several times broken your parole. If I hear another word, I shall lock you up, and will keep you on short rations until you are unable to talk at all. Our English officers are being so badly treated in Germany that I will make you pay for it."

It was a happy prospect. What could I do?

There were more than one thousand prisoners on board ship. The accommodation was the most appalling that I have ever witnessed. Without light or air the men sat huddled together under hatches, and their only physical exercise consisted in running up and down the narrow fore deck. When we were led into the room which had been prepared for us, I was horror-struck. I think I should have gone mad had I been obliged to stay there for long. Our English non commissioned officer seemed a sensible man. Through his kind offices I was able to secure for my friend, the locksmith, and myself a small cabin which even boasted of a porthole. Life on board was very monotonous. We rose at 6 a.m., and lights went out at 10 p.m.

In the mornings and the afternoons we had to stand about for two hours on the upper deck, and roll call was at noon. We took our meals in the huge dining rooms of the steamer. Twelve sat at one table, and I had to take my turn at waiting, fetch the food from the caboose for the mess, and wash the dirty crockery with the others.

M—, our Commandant, as a civilian, had travelled for a whisky firm, and had made so much money in this capacity that he was able to buy a commission. One circumstance had especially enraged him; as soon as we arrived we were asked which of us wished to pay 2.50 marks daily, for which consideration we would be allowed to take our meals separately, get better food, and be excused from washing our crockery. Of course we all saw through this rank swindle, and it made M— specially mad that we did not accept. On the second day I finished my report for the English Government, and presented myself with it to Mr. M—. He burst into offensive sniggering.

"You know very well that I will not pass on your petition, and you can imagine what I shall do to it. In Germany our English generals are forced to drag ploughs over the fields; *you* are going to pay for it."

It was hopeless to persuade him of the absurdity of his allegations. Every evening, when making the rounds at bedtime, he made a special point of entering my room as well, turned on the light and said: "Still here?" Too childish!

One day fifty civilian prisoners were ordered by Mr. M— to scour the first class deck and clean the portholes. Of course we went on strike. When Ave persisted in our refusal we were punished by being twice deprived of our dinner and having to go to bed at 9 p.m. Moreover, M— was such a coward that he did not dare muster us and order our punishment himself, but remained at a safe distance and sent his non commissioned officer as official delegate.

M— foamed with rage.

"Of course," he said, "it is again the fault of this 'flying-man'; he is at the root of the whole trouble, and one of these fine days he will incite the whole crew to mutiny. But I will teach him a lesson, and bring him before a court martial."

I got fed up with this state of affairs, for I was totally innocent, so I wrote M— a very energetic letter, in which I expressed a hope that he was only a "temporary lieutenant," not a "temporary gentleman."

M— declared that he would have nothing further to do with the "flying-man", and as early as the next day a steamer came alongside and took me and some of my companions in misfortune from the *Andania* and its vulgar jailer.

How relieved I felt! The train carried us westwards for many hours. Of course I was again alone in my compartment, accompanied not only by three non commissioned officers, but by an officer as well.

In the evening we reached Dorchester, where I was greeted by a totally different atmosphere. An English captain (whose name was Mitchell) from the prisoners' camp approached me and asked politely whether I was an officer.

"Yes."

"In this case I am surprised that you should have been brought to a soldiers' camp. Please forgive me if I cannot have you escorted by an officer. But my senior sergeant major will come with you. Will you kindly walk alone behind the other prisoners."

I was speechless.

As we were marching through this delightful, clean little town, I suddenly heard "The Watch on the Rhine" being sung behind us loudly, gaily, and with zest, followed by the most beautiful soldier songs, and then "O Germany, high in honours!" We thought we were dreaming, but when we looked round with amazement we saw a troop of about fifty German soldiers who had been commandeered from the camp to the station to fetch our luggage.

Oh, how our hearts beat! In the midst of enemies, in spite of wounds and captivity, this flaming enthusiasm, this rapturous singing! I must confess that the English were extraordinarily tolerant, and the population always behaved in exemplary fashion. Silently, closely pressed together, they stood on both sides of the street. From all the windows fair little heads peeped at us, but not one contemptuous gesture, not one abusive word. They even seemed to enjoy listening to the old German melodies.

In camp thirty civilian prisoners were allotted a small wooden hut, which combined our bed, dining and sitting room. A tiny palliasse, which lay on the floor, and two blankets made up our sleeping accommodation. My captain begged me to put up with existing conditions, as he was unfortunately unable to give me a special room to myself.

The camp at Dorchester contained 2000 to 3000 prisoners and consisted partly of old race horse stables and of wooden barracks. A hundred years ago German Hussars had been quartered in these same barracks, on the occasion of the visit of Field Marshal Blücher!

The prisoners were extremely comfortable, as the food was good and plentiful, the treatment irreproachable, and there were many opportunities for sport.

Captain Mitchell and Major Owen especially deserved praise for the treatment of our men. Both were true old regulars, had been through many campaigns and battles, and knew how to handle troops. These two and the English Medical Officer presented the men with games, gymnastic outfits and a band, and did whatever they could for them. Special praise is due to the senior German prisoner, a Warrant Officer, from Munich. He was a merchant, and spoke English fluently. A most remarkable personality. He was really the soul and veritable guardian angel of the camp. Nothing was done without his approval and directions. He was the English Camp Commandant's right hand man, and without him I do not know what would have become of the English, who did not possess the slightest vestige of talent for organization. It was simply extraordinary how this Warrant Officer looked after our people and acted as go-between with the English. The English officers knew full well what a help he was to them. By the way, after my arrival in Dorchester, I had already sent in my petition to be transferred to an officers' camp, for I knew that Mr. M— had kept back my former one. After a fortnight it was returned from the War Office with the remark that the name of some one in England who knew me must be given. This was most unwelcome; but finally I wrote to my English acquaintances, and in as soon as three days I received their answer that they would willingly vouch for my identity. The papers again went to the War Office, and I patiently waited for my transfer.

But time passed, and I still remained at Dorchester, and when, a fortnight after our arrival, the other civilian prisoners were again moved to another destination, I was able to arrange that I should remain in the soldiers' camp at Dorchester. However, I left my hut and moved into a small room over the stables, where I was warmly received by Sergeant Major N.

Life in this small room was unique and full of intimate comradeship. My colleagues were, apart from N., a huge Bavarian infantry soldier of the Body Guards Regiment, whose nickname was "Schorsch", and who acted as our cook; a nimble and clever private in the Hussars from Lorraine, a policeman by profession; and also two splendid rifle guards of gigantic stature, genuine blond Frisians. After a week we received a seventh guest. This was the sub-lieutenant H., the observer whom the English had fished out of the North Sea with his pilot, after they had been drifting about on the wrecked machine for over forty hours.

The comradeship in this room was ideal. The men had all been taken prisoners at the great retreat of the Marne, and, as was to be expected, these splendid fellows had only fallen into the enemy's hands when severely wounded. They were of such fine disposition, and showed such burning love for their country, that my heart filled with pride and satisfaction. The evenings were especially pleasant. We contrived a rough game with a board and some pieces of cork, and gambled on *petits chevaux* regularly every night with childish delight.

But the real fun began when we started exchanging experiences. Everything was new to me, and I was happy to learn at last from first hand information of our splendid battle and triumphs.

Every afternoon 300 to 400 prisoners, of course closely guarded by English soldiers, were led out for their exercise, which took them into the lovely open country. I often accompanied them. All the time our soldier songs were sung; but with particular force and ecstasy when we marched through the town, going and returning, "The Watch on the Rhine" and "O Germany, high in honours!" Imagine 300 or 400 of our picked men, our victorious troops under General von Kluck! The English population behaved even then with the utmost restraint, and never uttered a word of abuse or a threat. The sergeant major told me of a very nice episode. When Major Owen and Captain Mitchell were appointed to the camp, their wives implored them not to go among the "Huns" without escort and without being heavily armed. The two old soldiers, however, kept their own counsel, and were – not devoured! After a time they suggested to their wives that they should visit the camp and convince themselves that the German soldiers were quite normal people and not monsters as portrayed by the press. Naturally, at first the ladies fainted away. But after much persuasion, and being assured of a bodyguard, they ventured upon entering their husbands' offices and watched the doings of the German soldiers. The news of the visit got about, and silently our male choir assembled under the windows and warbled forth its finest songs. I am told that the ladies were so deeply moved that they were unable to speak, and could not hold back bitter tears. From thence onwards they often came and showed much kindness to our men.

Another story also is very typical.

A new colonel came to the camp. On his first round he was armed to the teeth, and walked about between two soldiers with fixed bayonets, one in front and the other behind him. When he met the major and the captain, absolutely unarmed and unaccompanied, he reproached them severely for their carelessness.

But he soon improved.

One day this new Commandant sent for these two gentlemen, and said to them in a tone full of horror: "Can you imagine this? We have been sent some new prisoners, and it has been reported that they are full of lice! Such dreadful things can only happen to the Germans."

Captain Mitchell turned calmly to the Major:

"Do you remember, Owen, that we were so covered with lice during our last campaign that we simply could not move?"

The Colonel was aghast. I must point out that though the Colonel was a colonel he had never in his life had anything to do with military affairs. But that can only happen in England!

About the end of March I at last received news from my people. It was nearly nine months since I had heard from them. It is easy to picture my feelings when I held in my hands my first letter from home, hesitating to open it, for all my brothers and male relatives had been at the Front since July 1914. It informed me that they were still safe; but, on the other hand, my beloved little sister, my best pal, had died from the effects of the war.

Towards the end of March the order came that I should be recognized as an officer, and transferred to an officers' camp. My small bundle and my hockey stick were soon collected, and after a warm farewell to my comrades I marched to the station with Major Owen.

I found the fine tact of the old gentleman a very particular blessing. After a journey that lasted several hours we reached Maidenhead, near London, where I was received by another English officer. And here, oh, miracle, I also met dear old friends. Five shining gold coins which had been taken from the locksmith, Ernst Suse, were handed over to my new companion, and the latter was able to return them at once to me, as I was an officer once more. Oh, the joy of our reunion! A motor-car took us to the Officers' Camp, Holyport. The sentries presented arms, the wire fences were opened, and I found myself in the midst of a joyous crowd of comrades. Who could have imagined this change!

I again met those I had last seen at Kiao-Chow – the victors of Coronel, the few gallant survivors of the Falkland Islands. It is impossible to imagine our joy. The questions and answers! the excitement! And then the miraculous happened, for I was conducted to my dormitory, and there I actually saw six or eight beds, made up with white, clean sheets. I had been a prisoner for eight weeks, and these were the first beds I beheld. Can one understand the shy reverence with which I laid myself to rest that night?

In the beginning, I thought myself in Paradise, the more so as I was again being treated as a human being. I was once more amongst my comrades, and found my old friends, and was greatly stimulated thereby.

The treatment in the camp was good. The English Commandant was a sensible man, who tried to ease our existence. The building was an old military school, and 100 officers were imprisoned in the camp – eight to ten shared a dormitory, which was at the same time a sitting room. Apart from this, there was a number of mess, reading and dining rooms, in which we spent most of our time when we were not in the fresh air. The food was purely English, therefore hardly palatable to the majority of the Germans, but more than sufficient and of good quality. At the beginning we managed our own mess; but this, unfortunately, was forbidden later on by the War Office. During the day we were left comparatively alone. We were allowed to move freely among the buildings and in the garden. At ten in the morning there was roll call, and at ten in the evening "lights out" and rounds.

Of course we were not allowed to approach the barbed-wire entanglements which surrounded the whole place, and which were strictly guarded and illuminated night and day. Twice a day the gates were opened, and we passed between a lane of English soldiers to the sports ground, which lay about 200 yards away. Our games were wonderfully organized. Two splendid football and, above all, some perfect hockey fields, stood at our disposal, and we displayed such amazing form that even the English were impressed. It is superfluous to add that these fields were also surrounded by barbed wire and sentries.

A very pleasant feature was the bi-weekly appearance of an excellent tailor, and also of a haberdasher, who provided us with excellent hosiery and gave us the opportunity of renewing our wardrobe.

Our monthly pay amounted to 120 marks, of which sixty was put aside for our keep. We were permitted to spend the rest; also to receive money from home. The post worked without a hitch. Letters from Germany, as well as parcels, took from six to eight days, and arrived regularly. Conditions were less fortunate in regard to our own correspondence. Our weekly allowance consisted of two short notes, and how gladly would we have filled reams to our dearest at home! The post was the Alpha and Omega of our existence. We divided our whole day according to its delivery, and the temper of the camp was regulated by it.

Every morning saw the same spectacle. When the interpreter arrived with the letters everything was abandoned and forgotten. The English officer was surrounded by a silent crowd of waiting people. Each one's heart was filled with the burning wish to receive some token, some loving message from home. What joy when one's hopes were fulfilled, how great the sorrow and disappointment when they were shattered. In the latter case, we always said: "One more day lost." When, two months afterwards, I was back in Germany, and was asked on many sides what one could do to give pleasure to the prisoners, I always said: "Write, write as much as you can. What the prisoner longs for most are letters."

We lived in very close comradeship. In the evenings we sat in groups round the beautiful, large fireplaces, in which burned huge logs of wood. The conversation touched upon battles and victories, sorrow and death, and wild, adventurous happenings. We had many good books, and a string quartet as well as a choir added much to our entertainment.

We played many a joke, and when we had had a jolly good laugh we felt relieved for a time from the terrible oppression which captivity exercised on our spirits.

At the end of April our quiet existence was suddenly broken up.

One evening the order was received to transfer fifty officers to the Officers' Camp at Donington Hall. Excitement ran high, for no one wanted to leave; but neither entreaties nor opposition prevailed. We had to pack our trunks and march off. I was the only naval officer of the party and that, unfortunately, because the English Commandant of the camp considered the proximity of London too dangerous a temptation for me. My devoted friend, Siebel, an army flying officer, followed me, so at least we two of the same service remained together.

On the 1st of May, therefore, we moved off again. Motor cars took us to Maidenhead Station, where two reserved carriages were waiting for us. We remained undisturbed in our compartments; but the carriages themselves were strictly guarded.

For many hours we rolled northwards. At the stations people looked into our windows' curiously, but preserved a quiet demeanour. Sometimes an old woman, probably a suffragette, put out her unlovely tongue at us. At last in the afternoon we reached the station, Donington Castle, near Derby, where we had to fall in in squads. Guarded by sixty or seventy soldiers, we were marched off on the order "Quick march".

Outside the station we were greeted by a howling mob, composed of women and undersized lads and children, but few men. In France many of us had been accustomed to this undignified behaviour of the populace, but in England it was a new experience. The women and the girls, belonging to the lower classes, behaved like savages. Yelling and whistling, they ran alongside and behind us, and occasionally a stone or a lump of dirt hurtled through the air. But the majority were splitting with laughter and seemed to enjoy their antics tremendously. At the first turning a car came hooting behind us. At the wheel sat our Interpreter-officer, Mr. M—, a fat and supercilious individual, whom we were to know exhaustively later on. Mr. M— was out to create an impression, and he at once proceeded to do so by running over one of his own soldiers, who belonged to our escort. General uproar followed, in which every one took part. Lastly, two of our "Huns" sprang forward and rescued the unfortunate Tommy from under the wheels. Thereupon the fury of the women turned upon Mr. M—, who would have had a poor time of it if he had not speedily driven off. It is most regrettable that he was able to do so! However, this incident was quickly forgotten, and the crowd went on yelling. It became more and more unruly and dirt more and more plentiful, when suddenly four or five cows, placidly chewing, came ambling along and tried to pass us on both sides. What followed was so comical that we, as well as our Tommies, stood still and roared with laughter. On beholding the peaceful cows the brave Amazons shrieked despairingly, gathered up their skirts and ran! Ruthlessly the strong trampled on the weak, and in the twinkling of an eye a confused mass of women lay screaming and kicking in the ditches on both sides of the road.

After that we were left in peace and were allowed to proceed rapidly on our way.

All the time I sharply scrutinized our surroundings and noted different landmarks, which might possibly prove useful some day.

The sun burned down on us unmercifully, and we were bathed in perspiration when we at last reached our new home – Donington Hall.

Discipline held sway there.

The portals and wire fences opened before us; the whole guard turned out and presented arms; the Officer in Command and two lieutenants stood at the right wing, their hands raised in salute.

After we had been received by the Camp Commandant, we were distributed over the rooms, and I was lucky enough to secure, with four other comrades, amongst whom was my *fidus Achates* Siebel, a very nice little den.

Here, also, I met a large number of old friends. Some of the survivors of the *Blücher*, some from torpedo boat destroyers and small cruisers, and several flying men from the army and navy.

Donington Hall was the model prisoners' camp of England. To go by all we had read about it for weeks in English papers it should have been Paradise. Daily, long winded columns abused the Government for the luxury with which the German officers were housed. As usually happens, the strongest attacks were launched by women, and they even turned our ejection from Donington Hall into a feminist issue. Even Parliament had to take up this matter repeatedly. It was rumoured that the place was lavishly furnished, that we had several entertainment and billiard rooms, a private deer park; and even indulged in fox hunts, especially got up for our benefit.

None of this was true. Donington Hall was a large, old castle dating from the seventeenth century, surrounded by a lovely old park; but its rooms were completely bare, and its accommodation as primitive and scanty as possible. There was no trace of the other items – entertainment rooms or hunting. After our arrival the inmates numbered 120, and we were packed together like pickled herrings. One cannot imagine what would have happened if the camp had held its full complement – 400 to 500 officers – as our mess, kitchens and bathrooms, etc., were far from sufficient even as it was.

We loved the beautiful park most. Our residence was divided into two zones – *i.e.* in the so-called day and night boundaries. These areas were marked off by huge erections of barbed wire, which were partly charged with electricity, illuminated at night by powerful arc-lamps, and guarded sharply by sentries both day and night.

At six in the evening, after the principal roll call, the day boundary was closed, and only reopened the next day at eight. Life at Donington Hall was practically the same as at Holyport, with the difference that, thanks to the park, we had greater liberty of movement, could indulge in more sport, and had three tennis courts. The food here also was English, so that many did not like it; but it was very good. The English colonel was reasonable, and, although he often grumbled, and was at times rather inclined to make us feel his authority, he was a distinguished, intelligent man, and a perfect soldier, and that was the principal thing. He did all that lay in his power to lighten our hard lot, and took a special interest in our sports – which was all to the good.

He had a most obnoxious substitute in the person of the interpreter, Lieutenant M—, the motorist, who was a worthy counterpart of my friend M— of the *Andania* – not only "temporary lieutenant," but also "temporary gentleman." His family came from Frankfurt-on-the-Main; he was director of a strolling troupe before the war, and he did nothing to disguise his base disposition. I believe the English colonel regarded him with the utmost contempt, and the English sergeants, with whom we occasionally exchanged a few words in the canteen, begged us to believe that all English officers were not like this Mr. M—.

One evening, towards the end of June, we had a delightful adventure. Outside the barbed wire a herd of wild deer – roebucks and fawns – used to assemble in their hundreds, and ran about as tame as goats.

That evening, a darling little fawn, which had lost its mother, ran past the wire fence, and, attracted by our alluring calls, it cleverly wriggled through the defences into the camp. The fawn was surrounded and petted (the huntsmen growled), and lastly it was carried in triumph in the arms of a lieutenant into the batmen's room, where we intended to rear it.

God knows how M— heard of it. At any rate he sent for the German Camp Adjutant, and said in a voice that shook with anxiety: "Lieutenant S., is it true that there is an animal in the camp?"

"Yes, sir; an animal."

"Has it come in through the wire entanglements?"

"Yes; it simply crept through."

"Oh, this is dreadful!" remarked Mr. M—, and he seemed to lose his voice altogether. "I must at once see the hole through which the big beast has crawled. I am convinced that the German officers have cut the wire in order to escape. The animal must also be at once removed."

And so it happened.

And – this is no joke – twenty men from the guard with fixed bayonets were sent for. The solitary German soldier with the innocent tiny fawn was taken into their midst. On the order "Quick march" the whole procession moved to the inside door of the fence. The latter was opened, the twenty men with the German soldier and the fawn stepped into the intervening space, the so-called "ock", the inner portal, was carefully shut. Only then was the outer one opened, the soldier liberated the fawn, and after that the whole procession wended its way back.

Oh, Mr. M— what a laughing stock you made of yourself!

After that all the entanglements were carefully examined, and, though it was impossible to find the smallest cleft through which a man could have crept, M—could not quiet down for days.

Apart from the post, the arrival of newspapers represented the chief interest of the day. We were allowed to receive the *Times* and the *Morning Post* and, though they were nearly exclusively filled with Entente victories, we knew them so well after a short time that we could read between the lines, and were able to conjecture the real state of affairs with approximate correctness.

But what rage in the newspapers at the sinking of the *Lusitania*, and what anger when the Russians had to retire – of course only for strategic reasons! We had manufactured for ourselves several huge maps of the theatres of war, which were correct even to the slightest details, and each morning at eleven our "General Staff Officers" were hard at work moving the little flags. Often the English colonel himself stood in front of them and thoughtfully shook his head.

Chapter Twelve

The Escape

In time captivity became unbearable. Nothing relieved my gloom – neither letters, parcels forwarded from home by loving hands, the company of my friends, not even hockey, to which I devoted myself so strenuously that in the evenings I used to drop asleep half dead from fatigue.

It was all of no avail. At last the prisoners' disease – home sickness – held me in its grip, as it had held so many before me. The apathy of most dreadful despair, of entire hopelessness. Hopeless!

For hours I lay on the grass and stared with wide opened eyes into the sky, and my whole soul longed fiercely for the white clouds above, to wander off with them to the distant beloved country.

When an English airman soared quietly and securely in the blue firmament, my heart contracted with pain, and a wild, desperate longing set me shivering. My condition grew steadily worse. I became irritable and nervous, behaved brusquely towards my comrades and deteriorated visibly, both mentally and physically. This was quite unreasonable on my part, for I should have been satisfied that at least I had seen something of the hostilities, and had had many interesting experiences! So many fell wounded into the enemy's hands during the very first days of the war; but the most to be pitied were those who had come from America at the beginning of the war, forsaking all their goods and chattels, all they held dear, to serve their Fatherland, and had been made prisoners through English treachery, before they had had a chance of drawing the sword.

We were greatly depressed owing to our being deprived of war news from German sources and, though we naturally gave no credence to the lying reports of the English, yet, after a while, we felt the oppression of reading, week after week, nothing but abuse of Germany, tidings of defeats, revolution and famine over there. Uncertainty was our worst trial, and the announcement of Italy's mean betrayal hit us particularly hard.

What triumph in the English papers!

At last I was no longer able to bear it. Something had to be done if I were to be saved from despair.

Day and night I planned, brooded, deliberated how I could escape from this miserable imprisonment. I had to act with the greatest calm and caution if I hoped to succeed.

For hours together I walked up and down in front of different parts of the entanglements, whilst I unostentatiously examined every wire and every stake. For hours together I lay in the grass in the vicinity of some of those spots that seemed favourable, feigning sleep. But all the time I was closely watching every object and noting the ways and habits of the different sentries. I had already fixed upon the spot where I had decided to climb the barbed wire. Now the question remained how to make headway after this obstacle had been overcome. We possessed neither a map of England nor a compass, no time-table, no means of assistance of any kind. We were even ignorant of the exact location of Donington Hall. I knew the road to Donington Castle, for I had fixed it in my memory on the day of our arrival. I had also heard through an officer, who had been taken by car to Donington Hall from Derby, that the latter lay about 25 to 30 miles away to the north, and that he had passed a long bridge before the car turned into the village. Next I made friends with a nice old English soldier, whom I presented occasionally with a few cigars, and invited to a glass of beer in the canteen. After we had met several times I asked him whether he did not find it very tedious to be tied to Donington, and whether he sometimes had a change?

"Oh yes," he said, now and then he cycled to Derby to the cinema.

"What! Derby?" said I. "But that is too far for you. You are far too old for that!"

"Too old? I? No, sir! You don't know an English Tommy if you can say that. When I am on my bike, I can race any young fellow, and in three to four hours I am in Derby!"

I had learned enough for that day. The next week I again met my old friend. We exchanged greetings, and I pressed into his hands a couple of cigars which I always carried about with me, though I do not smoke.

"Hallo, Tommy!" I began suddenly. "I was talking yesterday with a brother officer. I swore that Derby lies to the north of us, and he insists that it is to the south. If I win, you will get a good big jug of beer."

My friend's eyes glistened joyously, and he assured me on his sacred oath that I had won, and that Derby most certainly lay to the north of Donington Hall.

Now I knew.

And then and there I resolved to make common cause with a naval officer, Oberleutnant Trefftz, who knew England and spoke English remarkably well.

The 4th of July 1915 had been chosen for our escape. We had rehearsed it in every detail and made all our preparations.

On the 4th of July, in the morning, we reported ourselves sick.

At the morning roll call, at ten o'clock, our names were entered on the sick list, and on its completion the orderly sergeant came to our room and found us ill in bed.

Everything was working well.

With the afternoon came the decision.

About 4 p.m. I dressed, collected all that I considered necessary for my flight, ate several substantial buttered rolls, and bade farewell to my comrades, especially to my faithful friend Siebel, who, unfortunately, I could not take with me as he was no sailor and did not speak English.

A heavy storm was in progress, and rain poured in torrents from grey skies. The sentries stood wet and shivering in their sentry boxes, and therefore nobody paid any attention when two officers decided to walk about in the park, in spite of the rain. The park contained a grotto, surrounded by shrubs, from which one could overlook its whole expanse and the barbed wire without oneself being seen.

This is where Trefftz and I crept in. We took a hurried leave of Siebel, who covered us with garden chairs, and we were alone. From now onwards we were in the hands of Providence, and it was to be hoped that Fortune would not forsake us.

We waited in breathless suspense. Minutes seemed like centuries, but slowly and surely one hour passed after another, until the turret-clock struck six in loud, clear chimes. Our hearts thumped in unison. We heard the bell ring for roll call, the command "Attention," and then the noisy closing of the day boundary. We hardly dared to breathe, expecting at any moment to hear our names called out. It was 6.30 and nothing had happened. A weight slipped from our shoulders. Thank God, the first act was a success. For during roll call our names had again been reported on the sick list and, as soon as the officers were allowed to fall out, two of our comrades raced back as swiftly as they could through the back entrance and occupied Trefftz's bed and mine. Therefore, when the sergeant arrived he was able to account satisfactorily for the two invalids. As everything was now in order, the night boundary was closed, as every night, and even the sentries withdrawn from the day boundary. Thus we were left to our own devices. The exceptionally heavy rain proved a boon to us, for the English soldiers generally indulged in all kinds of frolic in the evenings, and we might have easily been discovered.

The hours followed each other. We lay in silence; sometimes we nudged each other and nodded our heads joyfully at the thought that up to now all had gone so smoothly.

At 10.30 p.m. our excitement came to a head. We had to pass our second test. We clearly heard the signal "Stand to", and from the open window of my former room "The Watch on the Rhine" rang out sonorously. It was the concerted signal that all were on the alert.

The orderly officer, accompanied by a sergeant, walked through all the rooms and satisfied himself that no one was missing. By observations carried on for weeks I had made sure that the orderly officers always chose the same route in order to return to their quarters, after their rounds, by the shortest way. So it was tonight. The round began with the room from which Trefftz was missing. Of course his bed was already occupied by some one. "All present?"

"Yes, sir!"

"All right! Goodnight, gentlemen."

And so forth. As soon as the orderly officer had turned the corner, two other comrades ran in the opposite direction and into my room, so that here also all could be reported "present".

It is difficult to conceive our excitement and nervous tension whilst this was in progress. We followed all the proceedings in our minds, and when suddenly silence supervened for an unconscionably lengthy period we feared the worst. With ice cold hands, ears on the alert for the slightest sound, we lay, hardly daring to breathe.

At last, at 11 p.m., a lusty cheer broke the stillness. It was our concerted signal that all was clear!

Chapter Thirteen

Black Nights on the Thames

All was silent around us. The rain ceased. The park lay wrapped in darkness, and only the light of the huge arc lamps, which lit up the night boundary, streamed faintly towards us. The dull sound of the sentries' footsteps as they paced up and down in front of their boxes, and their calls to each other every quarter of an hour, sounded uncanny in the stillness. At midnight the guard was changed, and I followed it with strained attention. Upon this, the orderly officer flashed his lamp over the day boundary, and at 12.30 a.m. quiet reigned again.

The moment for action had arrived. I crept softly as a cat from my hiding place, through the park up to the barbed wire fence, to convince myself that no sentries were about. When I saw that everything was in order and had found the exact spot where we wanted to climb over, I crawled back again to fetch Trefftz. Thereupon we returned by the same way.

When we reached the fence, I gave Trefftz my final instructions and handed him my small bundle.

I was the first to climb over the fence, which was about 9 feet high, and every 8 inches the wire was covered with long spikes.

Wires charged with electricity were placed 2½ feet from the ground. A mere touch would have sufficed to set in motion a system of bells that would, of course, have given the alarm to the whole camp. We wore leather leggings as protection against the spikes; round our knees we had wound puttees, and we wore leather gloves.

But all these precautions were of no avail, and we got badly scratched by the spikes. However, they prevented us from slipping and coming in contact with the electric wires. I easily swung myself over the first fence. Trefftz handed over our two bundles and followed me with equal ease.

Next we were confronted by a wire obstacle, 3 feet high by 30 feet wide, contrived according to the latest and most cunning devices. We ran over it like cats. After this we again came to a high barbed wire hedge, built on exactly the same lines as the first, and also electrically charged. We managed this too, except that I tore a piece out of the seat of my trousers, which I had to retrieve, in order to put it in again later.

But, thank God, we were over the boundary!

Trefftz and I clasped hands and looked at each other in silence.

But now the chief difficulty began. Cautiously we went forward in the darkness, crossing a stream, climbing over a wall, jumping into a deep ditch, and at last slunk past the guard house which stood at the entrance to the camp. Only after that were we in the open.

We ran without stopping along the wide main road which led to Donington Castle. After half an hour we stopped and took off our leggings and gloves, which had been slashed and torn by the wire. The palms of our hands, our feet, to say nothing of other parts of our body, were in a pretty condition. The barbed wire left us souvenirs which stung for weeks.

We now opened our bundles, took out civilian grey mackintoshes, and walked down the road in high spirits as if we were coming from a late entertainment. When Donington Castle came in sight, we had to be particularly careful. We had agreed upon all we would do in case we met anyone.

Suddenly, just as we were turning into the village, an English soldier came walking towards us. Trefftz embraced me, drew me towards him, and we behaved like a rollicking pair of love-birds. The Englishman surveyed us enviously, and went on his way, clicking his tongue. Only then, something in the stocky, undersized figure made me realize that it was the sergeant major of our camp! We stepped out briskly, and after passing the village we were favoured by chance and came upon the bridge about which we had been told. But we were at once confronted with a critical proposition. The highway branched off here in three directions, and it was impossible to get any further without knowledge of the road. At last, in spite of the darkness, we discovered a signpost – an extreme rarity in England. Luckily it was made of iron and, when Trefftz had climbed it, he was able to feel with his fingers the word "Derby" traced on it in raised letters.

We now fell into a quick step and, taking our bearings by the Polar star, swung along vigorously. Whenever we came across pedestrians and cars, and especially when the latter drove behind us, we hid in the ditch and waited until the danger was past. It was quite natural that we should surmise the presence of a messenger of Nemesis, ready to swoop down upon us, in any car that came along. When we were hungry we ate a little of the ham and chocolate we had brought with us. Unfortunately, the one was too salt and the other too sweet, so that we were plagued by an unquenchable thirst which soon became so unbearable that we could hardly advance. Matters were made worse as we had perspired freely during our exertions, and now we could find no better means of slaking our thirst than by standing in the ditch and licking the raindrops from the leaves, until we found a dirty little pool, on which we threw ourselves with avidity. And wasn't it good!

Gradually dawn came. About four in the morning, when we arrived within sight of the first houses of Derby's suburbs, the sun rose in majestic splendour, like a crimson ball on the horizon. We stood enraptured by this glorious spectacle, and we again shook hands and joyously waved to the sun.

For he came from Germany, straight from our country; he had caught his red hues from the red battlefields, and brought us faithful messages from our beloved ones. A good omen!

We now crept into a small garden and made an elaborate toilet. A clothes brush performed miracles, and a needle repaired the damage done to my trousers. The lack of shaving soap was remedied by spittle, after which our poor faces were subjected to the ministrations of a Gillette razor. We each sported our solitary collar and tie, leaving the brush as well as other unnecessary impedimenta behind us. We entered Derby, looking veritable "Knuts".

Our luck endured, and not only did we soon find the station, where we separated unobtrusively, but we also learned that the next train for London was leaving in a quarter of an hour. I took a third class return ticket to Leicester and, armed with a fat newspaper, boarded the train. At Leicester I got out, took a ticket to London, and when I entered the compartment I discovered, sitting opposite me, a gentleman clad in a grey overcoat, whom I must have met previously, but of whom I naturally took no notice. I believe his name began with a T.

About noon the train reached London. When I passed the ticket collector I must admit that I did not feel quite comfortable, and that my hand shook a little. But nothing happened, and after a few minutes I was swallowed up in the vortex of the capital.

It was extremely fortunate that I had spent some time in London two years previously, and knew my way about. I visited four different restaurants in turn, where I stilled my hunger by eating moderately in each, so as to avoid comments on my ravenous appetite. After that I walked along the Thames, recalling all the streets, bridges and landing stages which I knew of yore, and took special note of the localities where neutral steamers were moored.

I had fondly imagined that conditions would be more favourable, and that I should at once be able to find a boat. But I now saw that all the wharves and the majority of the neutral steamers were strictly guarded and lay in the middle of the river. At this moment everything contributed to my depression: the strange surroundings, my insecurity at the start, when I imagined that every one knew who I was and could guess that I had escaped from Donington Hall; also the fatigue and excitement of the night before, and the feeling of utter loneliness in the immense, inimical city. I had also failed to get a newspaper with the shipping intelligence, and this was a bitter disappointment.

Was it to be wondered at that at seven o'clock in the evening I stood weary and downcast on the steps of St. Paul's Cathedral, waiting for Trefftz? I waited until nine, but no Trefftz appeared.

Convinced that Trefftz had already managed his escape on a friendly steamer, I dragged myself, totally exhausted, to Hyde Park which, to my further discomfiture, I found closed. What should I do now? Where should I sleep? I could not stay in the streets if I were to remain unnoticed, and I did not dare go to an hotel as I had no passport which, even for English people, had become compulsory, and without which no hotel proprietor was allowed to receive visitors.

In a miserable bar, which I had entered to fortify myself, I was only able to get warm stout and one piece of cake. Everything else had been consumed, and when the bar closed I was again on the street. I turned into an aristocratic lane where beautiful mansions were surrounded by carefully tended gardens. I was hardly able to stand on my feet, and at the first favourable moment I jumped with quick decision over one of the garden fences and hid myself in a thick box hedge, only a foot away from the pavement. It is difficult to describe my state of mind. My pulses were hammering, and thoughts raced wildly through my tired brain. Wrapped in my mackintosh, I lay in my hiding-place, stealthily – like a thief.

If anyone had found me here in this dreadful situation – me, a German officer! I felt like a criminal, and in my heart I was firmly resolved never to disclose to anyone the details of my despicable adventure. Oh, had I known then where I should soon have to hang about at night, and even find nothing odd in it, I should have felt my position less keenly!

After I had lain for about an hour in my refuge, the French window of the house, leading to a beautiful veranda, opened, and several ladies and gentlemen in evening dress came out to enjoy the coolness of the night. I could see them and hear every word. Soon the sounds of a piano mingled with those of a splendid soprano voice, and the most wonderful songs of Schubert overwhelmed my soul with longing.

At last total exhaustion prevailed, and I slept heavily, seeing in my mind the most beautiful pictures of the future.

Next morning I was awakened by the regular heavy tread of a policeman who marched up and down the street, quite close to where I lay, with the bright, warm rays of the sun shining down upon me.

So after all I had overslept – it behoved me to be careful. The policemen ambled idiotically up and down without dreaming of departure. At last fortune favoured me. An enchanting little lady's maid opened the door, and hey presto! the policeman was at her side, playfully conversing with the pretty dear.

Without being seen by either, with a quick motion I vaulted over the fence into the street. It was already six o'clock, and Hyde Park was just being opened. As the Underground was not yet running, I went into the Park and dropped full length on a bench, near to other vagabonds who had made themselves comfortable there. I then pulled my hat over my face and slept profoundly until nine o'clock.

With fresh strength and courage I entered the Underground, and was carried to the harbour area. In the Strand huge, yellow posters attracted my attention, and who can describe my astonishment when I read on them, printed in big, fat letters, that:

(1) Mr. Trefftz had been recaptured the evening before; (2) Mr. Plüschow was still at large; but that (3) the police were already on his track.

The first and the third items were news; but I knew all about the second. I promptly bought a newspaper, went into a tea-shop, where I read with great interest the following notice:

"Extra Late War Edition

"HUNT FOR ESCAPED GERMAN

"*High-pitched Voice as a Clue*"

"Scotland Yard last night issued the following amended description of Gunther Plüschow, one of the German prisoners who escaped from Donington Hall, Leicestershire, on Monday:

Height, 5 feet 5½ inches; weight, 135lb.; complexion, fair; hair, blond; eyes, blue; and tattoo marks: Chinese dragon on left arm.

As already stated in the Daily Chronicle, Plüschow's companion, Trefftz, was recaptured on Monday evening at Millwall Docks. Both men are naval officers. An earlier description stated that Plüschow is twenty-nine years old. His voice is high-pitched.

"He is particularly smart and dapper in appearance, has very good teeth, which he shows somewhat prominently when talking or smiling, is 'very English in manner', and knows this country well. He also knows Japan well. He is quick and alert, both mentally and physically, and speaks French and English fluently and accurately. He was dressed in a grey lounge suit or grey-and-yellow mixture suit."

Poor Trefftz! So they had got him! I was clear in my mind as to what I was going to do, and the warrant gave me some valuable points. First, I had to get rid of my mackintosh. I therefore went to Blackfriars Station and left my overcoat in the cloakroom. As I handed the garment over, the clerk suddenly asked me: "What is your name, sir?" This question absolutely bowled me over, as I was quite unprepared for it. With shaking knees I asked: "Meinen?" (mine), answering in German as I naturally presumed that the man had guessed my identity.

"Oh, I see, Mr. Mine – M-i-n-e," and he handed me a receipt in the name of Mr. Mine. It was a miracle that this official had not noticed my terror, and I felt particularly uncomfortable when I had to pass the two policemen who stood on guard at the station, and who scrutinized me sharply.

I had escaped in a dark blue suit which had been made in Shanghai and worn in quick succession by Messrs. Brown and Scott, by the

EXTRA LATE WAR EDITION

HUNT FOR ESCAPED GERMAN.

HIGH - PITCHED VOICE AS A CLUE.

Scotland Yard last night issued the following amended description of Gunther Pluschow, one of the two German prisoners who escaped from Donington Hall, Leicestershire, on Monday :—

Height, 5ft. 6½in.; weight, 135lb.; complexion, fair; hair, blonde; eyes, blue; and tattoo marks, Chinese dragon on left arm.

As already stated in "The Daily Chronicle," Pluschow's companion, Treppitz, was recaptured on Monday evening at Millwall Docks. Both men are naval officers. An earlier description stated that Pluschow is 29 years old. His voice is high-pitched.

He is particularly smart and dapper in appearance, has very good teeth, which he shows somewhat prominently when talking or smiling; is "very English in manner," and knows this country well. He also knows Japan well. He is quick and alert, both mentally and physically, and speaks French and English fluently and accurately. He was dressed in a grey lounge suit or grey and yellow mixture suit.

London Prisoner Recaptured.

August Arndt, who escaped from internment at the Alexandra Palace, North London, on Sunday, has been recaptured.

Facsimile of notice in the *Daily Chronicle* after the escape.

millionaire MacGarvin and then by the locksmith, Ernst Suse, then again falling on better days when donned by a German naval officer, and now concluding its existence on the body of the dock labourer, George Mine. Under the coat I wore a blue sailor's jersey which a naval prisoner had given to me at Donington Hall. In my pocket I carried a tattered old sports cap, a knife, a small looking glass, a shaving set, a bit of string and two rags which represented handkerchiefs. In addition, I was the proud possessor of a fortune of 120 shillings which I had partly saved and partly borrowed; but never, either then or later, did I possess papers or passports of any kind.

I now sought a quiet, solitary spot. My beautiful soft hat fell accidentally into the river from London Bridge; collar and tie followed suit from another spot; a beautiful gilt stud held my green shirt together. After that a mixture of vaseline, bootblack and coal dust turned my blond hair black and greasy; my hands soon looked as if they had never made acquaintance with water; and at last I wallowed in a coal heap until I had turned into a perfect prototype of the dock labourer on strike – George Mine.

In this guise it was quite impossible to suspect me of being an officer, and "smart and dapper" were the last words anyone could have possibly applied to me. I think that I played my part really well, and, after I had surmounted my inner repulsion against the filth of my surroundings, I felt safe for the first time. I was in a position to represent what I intended to be – a lazy, dirty bargee, or a hand from a sailing ship.

Chapter Fourteen

Still at Large: The Chinese Dragon Clue

Gunther Plüschow, the German Naval-lieutenant, fugitive from Donington Hall, has now been at large seven days. The Chinese dragon tattooed on his left arm while on service in the East should, however, betray his identity.

> "Further particulars of the escape with Lieutenant Trefftz, who was caught at Millwall Docks within twenty-four hours, show that last Sunday evening a violent thunderstorm raged over Donington Hall when the evening roll call was taken. Instead of assembling with the other prisoners within the inner of the two rings of wire entanglements, the two hid within the outer circle. Their names were answered by other prisoners. A wooden plank near the outer ring showed how they got across the barbed wire."

[Notice circulated in the Press one week after the escape.]

For days I loafed about London, my cap set jauntily at the back of my head, my jacket open, showing my blue sweater and its one ornament, the gilt stud, hands in pocket, whistling and spitting, as is the custom of sailors in ports all the world over. No one suspected me, and my whole plan hinged on this, for my only safeguard against discovery lay in the exclusion of even the slightest suspicion directed

PLUSCHOW STILL FREE.

THE CHINESE DRAGON CLUE.

Gunther Pluschow, the German naval lieutenant, fugitive from Donington Hall, has now been at large seven days.   The Chinese dragon tattooed on his left arm while on service in the East should, however, betray his identity.

Further particulars of the escape with Lieutenant Treppitz, who was caught at Millwall Docks within twenty-four hours, show that last Sunday evening a violent thunderstorm raged over Donington Hall when the evening roll-call was taken. Instead of assembling with the other prisoners within the inner of the two rings of wire entanglement, the two hid within the outer circle.   Their names were answered by other prisoners.   A wooden plank near the outer ring showed how they got across the barbed wire.

Facsimile of notice circulated in the press a week after the escape.

against myself. If anyone had paid even passing attention to me, if a policeman had asked me for my name, I could only have given my own. Therefore, it was quite superfluous that the warrants put such stress on the tattoo marks on my arm as a clue to my identity. If matters had got thus far, it would have meant that the fight was over. On the second morning I had colossal luck! I sat on the top of a bus, and behind me two business men were engaged in animated conversation. Suddenly I caught the words, "Dutch steamer – departure – Tilbury," and from that moment I listened intently, trying to quell the joyful throbbings of my heart. For these careless gentlemen were recounting nothing less than the momentous news of the sailing, each morning at seven, of a fast Dutch steamer for Flushing, which cast anchor off Tilbury Docks every afternoon.

In the twinkling of an eye I was off the bus. I rushed off to Blackfriars Station, and an hour later was at Tilbury. It was midday, and the workmen were streaming into their public houses. First I went down to the river and reconnoitred; but my boat had not yet arrived. As I still had some time before me and felt very hungry, I went into one of the numerous eating houses specially frequented by dock-labourers. In a large room a hundred of them were gathered around long tables, partaking of huge meals. I followed their example, and, by putting down 8d., received a plate heaped with potatoes, vegetables and a large piece of meat. After that I purchased a big glass of stout from the bar and, sitting down amongst the men with the utmost unconcern, proceeded with my dinner, endeavouring to copy the table manners of the men around me, and nearly coming to grief when trying to assimilate peas with the help of a knife.

In the midst of my feast I suddenly felt a tap on the shoulder. Icy shivers ran down my back. The proprietor stood behind me and asked me for my papers. I naturally understood that he meant my identity book, and gave all up as lost. As I was unable to produce them, I was obliged to follow him, and saw to my dread that he went to the telephone. I was already casting furtive glances at the door and thinking how I could best make my escape, when the publican, who had been watching me through the glass door, returned and remarked: "If you have forgotten your papers, I can't help you. By the by, what is your name? And where do you come from?"

"I am George Mine, an American, ordinary seaman from the four-masted barque *Ohio*, lying upstream. I just came in here and have paid for my dinner, but of course haven't got my papers about me."

He remarked: "This is a private, social democratic club, and only members are allowed to eat here – you ought surely to know that – but if you become a member, you are welcome to come as often as you like."

Of course I agreed at once to his proposal, and paid three shillings' entrance fee. A bit of glaring red ribbon was passed through my buttonhole, and thus I became the latest member of the social democratic trades union of Tilbury!

I returned to my table as if nothing had happened, gulped down my stout to fortify myself after the shock I had just had, but also soon left for, to be quite frank, I had lost all my appetite and no longer cared for my food.

I now went down to the riverside, threw myself on to the grass, and, feigning sleep,1 kept a lynx-eyed watch.

Ship after ship went by, and my expectations rose every minute. At last, at 4 p.m., with proud bearing, the fast Dutch steamer dropped anchor and made fast to a buoy just in front of me. My happiness and my joy were indescribable when I read the ship's name in white shining letters on the bow: *Mecklenburg*.

There could be no better omen for me, since I am a native of Mecklenburg-Schwerin. I crossed over to Gravesend on a ferry boat, and from there unobtrusively watched the steamer. I adopted the careless demeanour and rolling gait of the typical Jack Tar, hands in my pockets, whistling a gay tune, but keeping eyes and mind keenly on the alert.

This was my plan: to swim to the buoy during the night, climb the hawser, creep on deck and reach Holland as a stowaway.

I soon found the basis for my operations.

After I had ascertained that nobody was paying attention to me, I climbed over a pile of wood and rubbish and concealed myself under some planks, where I discovered several bundles of hay. These afforded me a warm resting place, of which I made use on that and the following nights.

About midnight I left my refuge. Cautiously I clambered over the old planks and the litter strewn over the ground. The rain came down noisily and, though I had taken my bearings during the day, it was almost impossible in the pitch dark night to find the two barges which I had seen near the lumber pile.

Creeping on all fours, listening with straining ears and trying to pierce the surrounding blackness, I came closer to my object.

However, I perceived with dismay that the two barges which, in daytime, had been completely submerged, lay high and dry. Luckily, at the stern, a little dinghy rode on the water.

With prompt resolution I wanted to rush into the boat, but before I knew where I was I felt the ground slipping from under my feet and I sank to the hips into a squashy, slimy, stinking mass. I threw my arms about, and was just able to reach the plank, which ran from the shore to the sailing-boat, with my left hand.

It took all my strength to get free of the slime which had nearly proved my undoing, and I was completely exhausted when I at last dragged myself back to my bed of hay.

When the sun rose on the third morning of my escape, I had already returned to a bench in Gravesend Park, and was watching the *Mecklenburg* as she slipped her moorings at 7 a.m. and made for the open sea.

All that day, as well as later on, I loafed about London. For hours, like so many other wastrels, I watched from the bridges the position of the neutral steamers, the loading and unloading of cargoes, noting their stage and progress, in order, if possible, to take advantage of a lucky moment to slip on board.

I fed all these days in some of the worst eating houses of the East End. I looked so disreputable and dirty, often limping or reeling about like a drunkard, and put on such an imbecile stare that no one bothered about me. I avoided speech, and sharply observed the workmen's pronunciation and the way in which they ordered their food. Soon I had acquired such facility and quickness – to say nothing of amazing impudence – that I no longer even considered the possibility of being caught. In the evening I returned to Gravesend.

This time a new steamer lay at anchor in the river, the *Princess Juliana*.

I now proceeded to pay still more attention to the conformation of the riverside, so as to safeguard myself against further accidents.

At midnight I found myself at the spot I had chosen. The bank was stony and the tide just going out. I quietly discarded my jacket, boots and stockings, stowed the latter, with my watch, shaving-set, etc., in my cap, and put it on, fastening it securely on my head.

After that I hid the jacket and the boots under a stone, tightened the leather belt which held my trousers, and, dressed as I was, slipped gently into the water and swam in the direction of the boat.

The night was rainy and dark. Soon I was unable to recognize the shore which I had just left, but could just make out the outline of a rowing boat which lay at anchor. I made for it, but in spite of terrible exertions could not get any nearer. My clothes were soaked through, and, growing heavier and heavier, nearly dragged me down. My strength began to abandon me, and so strong was the current that other rowing boats that lay at anchor seemed to shoot past me like phantoms. Swimming desperately and exerting all my strength, I tried to keep my head above the water.

Soon, though, I lost consciousness, but when I recovered it, I lay high and dry on some flat stones covered with seaweed.

A kind fate had directed me to the few stony tracts of the shore where the river makes a sharp bend, and, thanks to the quickly outflowing tide, I lay out of the water.

Trembling and shivering with cold and exertion, I staggered along the river bank and after an hour I found my jacket and my boots. After that I climbed over, my fence and lay down, with chattering teeth, on my couch of straw.

It was still pouring, and an icy wind swept over me. My only covering consisted of my wet jacket and my two hands, which I spread out protectively over my stomach so as to try at least to keep well and going for the next few days. After two hours, being quite unable to sleep, I got up and ran about to get a little warmer.

My wet clothes only dried when they had hung over a stove a few days later in Germany! I again went to London for the day. I hung around in several churches, where I probably created the impression that I was praying devoutly; in reality I enjoyed an occasional nap there.

Another notice:

"Much-escaped Fugitive
"Plüschow's Aeroplane Flight from Tsing-Tao

"By the Chinese dragon clue the authorities still hope to trace Lieutenant Gunther Plüschow, of the German Navy, who escaped from Donington Hall on Monday. The dragon is tattooed on the fugitive's left arm in Oriental colours. It was probably worked by a native artist, for although but twenty-nine years of age, Plüschow has had an adventurous career in the Kaiser's Navy.

"He was in Tsing-Tao when the British and Japanese besieged that German fortress. Shortly before it fell, Plüschow escaped in an aeroplane, and some weeks later he was found on board a Japanese trading ship at Gibraltar.

"He will probably endeavour to sign on as a seaman in a neutral ship sailing from a British port and, with this in view, a very careful watch is being kept at all ports throughout the country. Plüschow is a typical sailor, about 5 feet 6 inches in height, with fair hair and fresh complexion. He would pass for a Dutchman with his broken English. Nothing he can do can remove the Chinese dragon from his left arm, and his recapture should be but a matter of time."

On that day I nearly became an English soldier. On one of the platforms, erected in the midst of a public square, I saw an orator standing up and addressing the people—of course, angling for recruits. In the most brilliant colours, and with the highest enthusiasm, he depicted to the attentive crowd the entrée into London of victorious German troops. "The streets of London," he said, "will re-echo to the tread of the 'Huns'; your wives will be ravished by German soldiers and trampled on by their muddy boots. Will you allow this, free Britons?" An indignant "No" sounded back. "Very well, then – come and join the army now!"

I expected a general rush forward, for the man had spoken most impressively; but no one budged, no one volunteered, or believed that Kitchener specially wanted *him*. The orator now started all over again, but his flaming words fell on deaf ears.

In the meantime, English recruiting sergeants moved about the crowd. Everywhere people shook their heads. Not one of Albion's valorous sons was having any. Suddenly my turn came.

A sergeant as tall as a lamp post stood before me and felt the biceps of my forearms. He seemed very pleased with his examination, for he tried to convince me by all the means in his power that to be a soldier in Kitchener's army was the most beautiful thing in the world. I refused. "No," I said; "it is quite impossible. I am only seventeen."

"Oh, that don't matter; we shall simply turn it into eighteen, and that'll be all right."

"No, really, it's quite impossible. Moreover, I am an American, and have no permission from my Captain." The persistent fellow now produced an oleograph on which the English uniforms were depicted in the, gaudiest colours. He simply would not let me go. To get rid of him I asked him to leave it with me, and promised to talk it over with my skipper, and to tell him next day which uniform I preferred. It goes without saying that I always made a great detour round this place.

I had by then acquired so much confidence that I walked into the British Museum, visited several picture galleries and even frequented matinées at music halls, without being asked questions. The pretty blonde attendants at the music halls were especially friendly to me, and seemed to pity the poor sailor who had wandered in by chance. What amused me most was to see the glances of disgust and contempt which the ladies and the young girls used to throw at me on the top of the buses. If they had known who sat near them! Is it surprising that I should not smell sweetly considering my night's work and the wet and slimy state of my clothes? In the evening I was back at Gravesend. In the little park which overlooked the Thames I listened quietly for hours to the strains of a military band. I had definitely given up my plan to swim to the steamer, for I saw that the distance was too great and the current too strong. I decided, therefore, to commandeer unobtrusively, somehow, a dinghy in which to reach the steamer. Just in front of me I saw one which I deemed suitable for my purpose, but it was moored to a wharf over which a sentry stood guard by day and night. But the risk had to be taken. The night was very dark when, about 12, I crept through the park and crawled up to the embankment wall, which was about 6 feet high. I jumped over the hedge and saw the boat rocking gently on the water. I listened breathlessly. The sentry marched up and down. Half asleep, I had taken off my boots, fastening them with the laces round my neck and holding an open knife between my teeth. With the stealth of an Indian I let myself down over the wall, and was just able to reach the gunwale of the boat with my toes. My hands slipped over the hard granite without a sound, and a second later I dropped into the boat, where I huddled in a corner, listening with breathless attention; but my sentry went on striding up and down undisturbed under the bright arc lamps. My boat, luckily, lay in shadow.

My eyes, trained through T.B.D. practice, saw in spite of the pitch darkness almost as well as by day. Carefully I felt for the oars. Damn! They were padlocked! Luckily the chain lay loose, and silently I first freed the boat-hook, then one oar after the other from the chain. My knife now sawed through the two ropes which held the boat to the wall, and I dipped my oars noiselessly into the water and impelled my little boat forward.

When I had .entered the boat, it had already shipped a good deal of water. Now I noticed to my dismay that the water was rapidly rising. It was already lapping the thwart, and the boat became more and more difficult to handle as it grew heavier and heavier. I threw myself despairingly on my oars. Suddenly, with a grinding noise, the keel grounded and the boat lay immovable. Nothing now was of avail, neither pulling nor rowing, nor the use of the boat-hook. The boat simply refused to budge. Very quickly the water sank round it, and after a few minutes I sat dry in the mud, but to make up for this the boat was brimful of water. I had never in my life witnessed such a change in the water-level due to the tide. Although the Thames is well known in this respect, I had never believed that possible.

At this moment I found myself in the most critical position of my escape. I was surrounded on all sides by slushy, stinking slime, whose acquaintance I had made two evenings before at the risk of my life. The very thought caused me to shudder. About 200 yards off the sentry marched up and down, and I found myself with my boat 15 feet from the 6 foot high granite wall.

I sat reflecting coolly. One thing appeared a sheer necessity – not to be found there by the English, who might have killed me like a mad dog.

But the water was not due to rise before the next afternoon. Therefore it behoved me to muster my energy, clench my teeth, and try to get the better of the mud. I slipped off my stockings, turned up my trousers as high as I could, then I placed the thwarts and the oars close to each other on the seething and gurgling ooze, used the boat-hook as a leaping-pole by placing its point on a board, stood on the gunwale, and, gathering all my strength to a mighty effort, I vaulted into space – but lay, alas, the next moment 3 feet short of the wall, and sank deep over knee into the clammy slush, touching hard bottom, however, as I did so. Now I worked myself along the wall, placed my boat-hook as a climbing-pole against it, and found myself in a few seconds on top, after which I slid into the grass of the park, where a few hours previously I had been listening to the music. Unbroken silence reigned around me. Unutterable relief flooded me, for nobody, not even the sentry, had noticed anything.

With acute discomfort I contemplated my legs. They were covered with a thick, grey, malodorous mass, and there was no water in the vicinity to clean them. But it was impossible to put on boots or stockings whilst they were in that condition. With infinite trouble I succeeded in scraping off the dirt as far as possible, and waited for the rest to dry; then only was I able to resume a fairly decent appearance.

My first plan had miscarried, but in spite of this I felt I had had such luck with it that I was ready to undertake a second venture.

I now made my way to the little bridge, which was guarded by my sentry, and, impersonating a drunken sailor, I reeled about until I gently collided with the good fellow. He, however, seemed quite used to such happenings, for remarking pleasantly, "Hallo, old Jack! One whisky too much!", he patted me on the shoulder and let me pass.

A hundred yards farther on, and I had regained my normal demeanour. After a short search I found the place from which I had started the night before on my ill-starred swimming attempt,

It was about 2 a.m., and in a trice I had undressed and sprang, agile and unhampered – as God had made me – into the water. For the first time the sky was covered with clouds, and the outlines of rowing boats, anchored at a distance of about 200 yards from the shore, appeared vague and shadowy. The water was quite unusually phosphorescent, and I have only observed it to that degree in the tropics. I swam, therefore, in a sea of gold and silver. At any other time I would have admired this play of Nature immensely, but now I only felt fear that my body would flash suspiciously white in this clear golden light. At the start, all went well. But as soon as I had passed the left bend of the river, where the shore afforded some protection, I was seized by the current, and had to fight for my life with the watery elements. As I was losing my strength I reached the first boat, made a final effort and hoisted myself noisily into it. Oh, persecution of a pitiless fate! The boat was empty – no scull, no boat-hook with which I could have put it in motion. After a short pause I again slipped into the water and drifted on to the next boat. And this, too, was empty! And the same happened with the three next. And when I reached the last one, after I had rested a little, I again dipped into the glittering but now unpleasantly cold water. Two hours after I had started on my adventure, I again reached the place where I had left my clothes.

As I was trembling like an aspen leaf with cold and exposure, I found it particularly hard to get into my sodden and sticky togs.

Half an hour later I was back in my sleeping-place amid the hay, beginning to feel serious doubts in the existence of my lucky star!

Could I be blamed if my spirits fell a little, and if I became quite indifferent to my interests? I confess I was so discouraged that the next morning I did not find sufficient energy to leave my hiding-place in time, and only escaped over my fence after the proprietor of the timber-pile had passed close in front of my retreat several times. That day I walked up to London on foot from Gravesend, and returned by the other side of the Thames to Tilbury. All this, in order to find a boat that I could purloin unnoticed. It was quite incredible that I could not do so; several lay there, as if waiting for me; but they were only too well guarded. I gave it up in despair.

That evening I went to a music hall, with the firm intention of blowing my last pound, and then staking everything on one card, and try to get to the docks and hide there on a neutral steamer. And if this plan miscarried – as it had with Trefftz – I decided to give myself up to the police.

I stood in the upper gallery of the biggest music hall in London and watched the performance. An inner voice whispered to me: "Your place is at Gravesend, working for your escape. Your duty is to throw off this slackness, otherwise you are not worthy to be a German sailor!"

So when I saw the *tableaux vivants*, scenes from the trenches and allegories of the coming Victory and Peace, in which the Germans naturally figured as fleeing and conquered, when at last, in the chief picture, Britannia appeared – a shining figure with the Palm of Victory in her hand, and a field-grey German soldier lying prostrate beneath her right foot – I felt consumed by a flame of righteous anger, and in spite of the forcible protests of my neighbours I fled from the theatre and was able to catch the last train to Tilbury.

Only then did I feel happy again. And I felt so certain now that my plan would come off, that no room was left for doubt.

After I had passed the first fishermen's huts of Gravesend, I found a small scull. I took it with me. In mid-stream, just near the landing-place of the fishing-vessels, a little dinghy bobbed on the water. Not more than twenty feet away sat their owners on a bench, so absorbed in tender flirtation with their fair ones that the good sea folk took no heed of my appearance on the scene.

It was risky, but "Nothing venture, nothing gained", I muttered to myself. And, thanks to my acquired proficiency, I crept soundlessly into the boat – one sharp cut, and the tiny nutshell softly glided alongside a fishing boat, on whose quarter deck a woman was lulling her baby to sleep.

As there were no rowlocks in the boat, I sat aft, and pushed off with all my strength from the shore. I had, however, hardly covered one-third of the distance, when the ebbtide caught me in its whirl, spun my boat round like a top and paralysed all my efforts

Gunther Plüschow in the disguise of a dock labourer,
in which he escaped.

at steering. The time had come to show my sailor's efficiency. With an iron grip I recovered control of the boat and, floating with the tide, I steered a downstream course. A dangerous moment was at hand. An imposing military pontoon bridge, stretching across the river, and guarded by soldiers, came across my way. Summoning cool resolution and sharp attention to my aid, looking straight ahead and only intent on my scull, I disregarded the sentry's challenge and shot through between the two pontoons. A few seconds after the boat sustained a heavy shock, and I floundered on to the anchor-cable of a mighty coal-tender. With lightning speed I flung my painter round it, and this just in time, for the boat nearly capsized. But I was safe. The water whirled madly past it, as the ebbtide, reinforced by the drop of the river, must have fully set in. I had now only to wait patiently.

My steamer lay to starboard. I wanted to bide my time until the flow of the tide made it possible for me to get across.

I was already bubbling over with cock sureness when the necessary damper was administered. Dawn was breaking, the outlines of the anchored ships became clearer and clearer. At last the sun rose, and still the water ran out so strongly that it was impossible even to contemplate getting away. Anyhow, it was impossible to carry out my flight just then. But at last, happy in the possession of the long desired boat, I slid downstream and, after an hour, pulled up at a crumbling old bridge on the right bank of the Thames. I pushed my boat under it, took both sculls with me as a precautionary measure, and hid them in the long grass. Then I lay down close to them, and at eight o'clock I saw my steamer, the *Mecklenburg*, vanishing proudly before my eyes. My patience had still to undergo a severe test. I remained lying in the grass for the next sixteen hours until, at eight o'clock that night, the hour of my deliverance struck.

I again entered my boat. Cautiously I allowed myself to be driven upstream by the incoming tide, and fastened my boat to the same coal tender near which I had been stranded the night before. Athwart to me lay the *Princess Juliana* moored to her buoy.

As I had time to spare, I lay down at the bottom of my boat and tried to take forty winks, but in vain. The tide rose, and I was once more surrounded by the rushing water.

At midnight all was still around me and when, at one o'clock, the boat was quietly bobbing on the flow, I cast off, sat up in my boat, and rowed with as much self-possession as if I had been one of a Sunday party in Kiel Harbour, to the steamer.

Unnoticed, I reached the buoy. The black hull of my steamer towered high above me. A strong pull – and I was atop the buoy. I now bade farewell to my faithful swan with a sound kick, which set it off downstream with the start of the ebb. During the next few minutes I lay as silent as a mouse. Then I climbed with iron composure – and this time like a cat – the mighty steel cable to the hawse. Cautiously I leaned my head over the rail and spied about. The forecastle was empty.

I jerked myself upwards and stood on the deck.

Chapter Fifteen

The Stowaway

I now crept along the deck to the capstan and hid in the oil save-all beneath the windlass. As all remained quiet, and not a soul hove in sight, I climbed out of my nook, took off my boots, and stowed them away under a stack of timber in a corner of the fore deck. I now proceeded to investigate in my stockinged feet. When I looked down from a corner astern the fore deck to the cargo deck I staggered back suddenly. Breathlessly, but without turning a hair, I remained leaning against the ventilator. Below, on the cargo deck, stood two sentries, who were staring fixedly upwards.

After I had remained for over half an hour in this cramped position, and my knees were beginning to knock under, there tripped two stewardesses from the middle deck. They were apparently coming off night duty

My two sentries immediately seized the golden moment, and became so absorbed in their conversation that they no longer paid any attention to what was going on around them.

The dawn was breaking, and I had to act at once if I was not to lose all I had achieved at such a price.

I let myself down along the counter on the side of the fore deck opposite to the two loving couples, and landed on the cargo deck. Without pausing for a moment I stepped out gently, glided past the two sentries, reached the promenade deck safely and, climbing up a deck pillar, found myself shortly afterwards on the out-board side of a life boat.

Holding on with one hand with a grip of iron, for the Thames was lapping hungrily not 12 yards away, with my other, aided by my teeth, I tore open a few of the tapes of the boat cover, and with a last output of strength I crept through this small gap and crouched, well hidden from curious eyes, into the interior of the boat.

And then, naturally, I came to the end of my endurance. The prodigious physical exertions, acute excitement, and last, but not least, my ravenous hunger, stretched me flat on the boards of the boat, and in the same moment I no longer knew what was going on around me.

Chapter Sixteen

The Way to Freedom

Shrill blasts from the siren woke me from a sleep which in its
dreamless-ness resembled death.

I prudently loosened the tapes of my boat-cover, and with
difficulty suppressed a "Hurrah!", for the steamer was running into
the harbour of Flushing.

Nothing mattered any longer. I pulled out my knife, and at one
blow ripped open the boat-cover from end to end; but this time on
the deck side.

With a deep breath, I stood in the middle of the boat deck, and
expected to be made a prisoner at any moment.

But no one bothered about me. The crew was occupied with
landing manoeuvres; the travellers with their luggage.

I now descended to the promenade deck, where several passengers
eyed me with indignation on account of my unkempt appearance
and my torn blue stockings, which looked, I must say, anything but
dainty.

But my eyes must have been so radiantly happy, and such joy
depicted on my dirty, emaciated features that many a woman glanced
at me with surprise.

I could no longer go about like this. I therefore repaired to the fore
deck, fetched my boots (my best hockey boots, kindly gifts from the
English) and, though a Dutch sailor blew me up gruffly, I calmly put
on my beloved boots and wandered off to the gangway.

The steamer had made fast directly to the pier.

The passengers left the ship, bidding farewell to the Captain and the ship's officers. At first I had intended to make myself known to the Captain, in order to avoid any trouble to the Dutch Steamship Company. But more prudent counsels prevailed, and with my hands in my pockets, looking as unobtrusive as I could, I slunk down the gangway.

Nobody paid any attention to me, so I pretended to belong to the ship's crew, and even helped to fasten the hawsers. Then I mixed with the crowd, and whilst the passengers were being subjected to a strict control I looked round, and near the railings discovered a door, on which stood in large letters "Exit Forbidden."

There, surely, lay the way to freedom! In the twinkling of an eye I negotiated this childishly easy obstacle, and stood without.

I was free!

I had to make the greatest effort of my life to keep myself from jumping about like a madman. Two countrymen of mine gave me a cordial welcome, though they would not believe that I was an officer, and, above all things, that I had achieved my escape from England.

How horrible the water in my bath looked!

I also ate enough for three that night.

After I had bought a few small necessaries the next day, I boarded a slow train for Germany, wearing workman's clothes.

As the train was going to start, a man came up behind me and tapped me on the shoulder (how I did hate this manner of greeting!) and asked me, " Where are your papers?"

"Who are you, anyway?" I said.

"I am Secret Service."

"Anybody can say that."

"Of course, sir; but here's my badge."

For a moment I felt dizzy. I explained to this gentleman with great suavity that I possessed no papers, that I was on my way back to Germany, and that I should give no trouble to the Dutch Government.

" So," he remarked, "you come from England, and you have no papers? I suppose that was a bit difficult?"

"Yes. Rather!" I said.

"Well, I wish you a further pleasant journey."

We shook hands as the train moved off.

Chapter Seventeen

Back in the Fatherland!

I was quite unable to sit still for long. Alone in my first class compartment I was overwhelmed by the thoughts and hopes which raced through my brain. I ran about my railway carriage like a wild animal in a cage.

At last! At last! It seemed an eternity; the train passed slowly over the German frontier.

The black and white post greeted my eyes and, leaning out of the window, I joyfully yelled "Hurrah!" twice.

But the third "Hurrah!" stuck in my throat, as carried away by gratitude, happiness and delight I sobbed aloud, and could not prevent the tears gushing from my eyes.

Was this sloppiness?

The train stopped at Goch. The first "field-greys" I had ever seen in my life stood on the platform as I jumped carelessly out of the train.

A harsh grip seized me by the collar, and a huge Prussian cavalry sergeant major, with fierce eyes under a shining helmet, held me in his iron fist.

"Ha! now we have got the young scamp!"

I would gladly have fallen on my dear "field-grey's" neck, for never had I felt safer in my life than at that moment.

I tried to explain who I was; but a smile which would have boded but little consolation to anyone else was all the answer I got.

Two brave Landsturm veterans conducted me to Wesel under arrest next morning.

No one was at the office yet to interview me. Small boys had followed me, throwing stones and shouting: "They have got him; they have got him – the spy!" The darling little blond heads!

An orderly received me!

"Sit down – you there. With people like you we don't lose much time. When the Herr Kapitänleutnant F. arrives, just a short examination – and up in the air you go."

After some little time the Redoubtable One appeared – of course a comrade of mine. Indescribable astonishment and joy! But the stupid face of my amiable orderly was good to behold. He had to run off straight away and fetch my breakfast.

I derived special satisfaction while still at Wesel from reading an English warrant from the *Daily Mail*, dated 12th July, when I was already safe, which ended by declaring that I would probably try to escape as a sailor on a neutral steamer and that: "His recapture should be but a matter of time."

An hour later I sat, still in my workman's clothes, a passport in my pocket, in the Berlin express – of course first class!

At last I had attained my goal! It had taken me nearly nine months to break my way through from Kiao-Chow to Germany.

Germany, oh, my beloved country! I had come back to thee!

The sun was shining radiantly on the 13th of July 1915, and my elated eyes were taking in the lovely pictures of my countryside.

I had settled down alone in my first class carriage, and had spread my belongings on both sides of the window, and begun to jot down my report in pencil.

At Münster an old general in full uniform entered my compartment. I stood up politely, cleared a seat, and said, "May I most humbly place this seat at Your Excellency's disposal?"

A furious look from his hard eyes, an outraged growl. "Brrrr," and the door slammed to. I was alone. If this little book should fall by chance into His Excellency's hands, may I be forgiven that I forgot, when addressing him, what clothes I was wearing at the time.

At seven o'clock that evening the train entered the Zoo Station.

A pair of wonderful blue eyes swimming in tears, a gorgeous bunch of crimson roses, and unable to utter a word through sheer happiness and the joy of reunion, we left the station.

I passed the next days as in a dream.

When I entered the Admiralty, the porter naturally would not allow me to come in; and also in the large shops, where I had to buy things in double quick time, as nothing was left me but my workman's attire, the commissionaires were bent on ejecting me.

I only worked a few days at the Imperial Naval Ministry, and then I received my Emperor's thanks.

And with the Iron Cross of the First Class I proudly went home to my people.

After a few weeks' rest I received my greatest reward.

I became a "flying-man" again, and was allowed to co-operate in the great work of Germany's fight and victory.

And when, at the Eastern Front, my most gracious Emperor and Master inspected the Naval Flying Station under my command, and shook hands with me and personally expressed his Imperial satisfaction, I looked straight into his eyes, and pressed in burning letters graven in my heart stood:

"With God for Emperor and Fatherland."

THE END